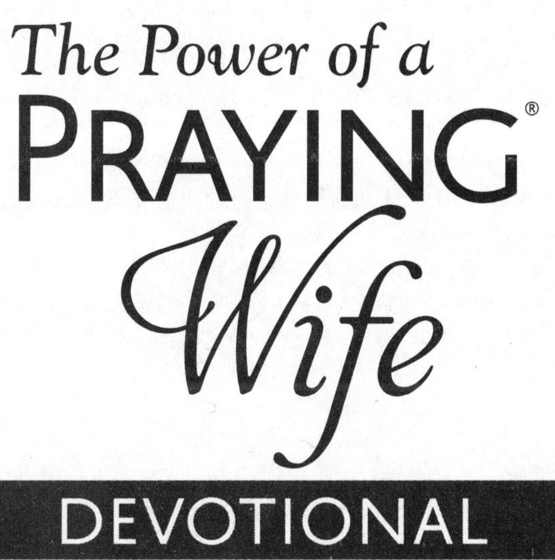

STORMIE OMARTIAN

HARVEST HOUSE PUBLISHERS
EUGENE, OREGON

Cover by Harvest House Publishers, Inc., Eugene, Oregon

Cover illustration © Komar art / Shutterstock

Back cover author photo © Michael Gomez Photography

THE POWER OF A PRAYING® WIFE DEVOTIONAL

Published by Harvest House Publishers
Eugene, Oregon 97402
www.harvesthousepublishers.com

ISBN 978-0-7369-5889-9 (Softcover)
ISBN 978-0-7369-5890-5 (eBook)

Printed in the United States of America

15 16 17 18 19 20 21 / BP-NI / 10 9 8 7 6 5 4 3

I will give you a new heart
and put a new spirit within you.

Ezekiel 36:26

Whatever things you ask in prayer,
believing, you will receive.

Matthew 21:22

CONTENTS

How Can This Praying Wife Devotional Help Me?

IF I HAD IT TO DO ALL OVER AGAIN, I would not write *The Power of a Praying® Wife* any differently than I did. However, in this new *The Power of a Praying® Wife Devotional*, I am sharing what the Lord has taught me about being a praying wife in the years since writing the earlier book.

First of all, I have included much more prayer in this book for you as a wife. In fact, one-third of the book consists of devotions and prayers for you to pray for *yourself*. A second third includes devotions and prayers for you to pray for your *husband*, and a last third has devotions and prayers for you to pray for your *marriage*. But I have not grouped these thirds separately into "me," "him, and "us" sections. I have, instead, alternated prayers for wife, husband, and marriage throughout the book so that every three devotions includes one of each—that is, one for you, one for your husband, and one for your marriage. The reason for that is I believe all three types of prayer are crucial to sustaining a solid marriage.

What you might not realize is how extremely important it is to pray for yourself as a wife. Women tend to neglect themselves in this way, and it is vital to your marriage not to do so. When you pray for yourself, you affect your spirit, soul, body, wholeness, insight, understanding, strength, and freedom in Christ more than you think. Personal prayer increases your ability to receive revelation from God. That's because, as you pray, God gives you the ability to see what is really going on in your own world and in the spirit realm. For example, you become aware of when your flesh may be dominating your spirit, or when the enemy of your soul is attempting to stir up strife and present his lies as truth. These things are crucial to you as a wife in being able to maintain a good, strong marriage—at least, as much as is dependent upon you.

All of this means you must still pray the "Change me, Lord" prayer. (I know that is not as much fun as praying the "Change *him*, Lord" prayer, but, unfortunately, that one seldom, if ever, is answered.) But now you have to take the "Change me, Lord" prayer to the next level and pray that God will show you everything you need to see about yourself. You must ask God to reveal what you should know and help you do what you need to do. For example, you can pray that God will enable you to keep worry, fear, doubt, and unclear thinking from getting in the way of your life and affecting what you do and say. God wants you to give *Him* control over your mind and heart. While He gave you the ability to feel, He doesn't want your feelings or emotions to rule you in a way that makes both you and your husband miserable. He wants you to bring all your feelings and emotions to Him—your Lord and confidant—and put them in the hands and under the control of the Holy Spirit. The devotions and prayers in this book will help you do that.

Another reason praying for yourself is important is because, as you grow older, you especially need the beauty of a quiet and gentle spirit. In order for that to happen, you must have the beauty of the Lord *in* you, beautifying every part of your inner-self—which affects the beauty of your outer-self more than anything else. A woman with a beautiful heart, soul, and mind is more attractive to everyone, but most importantly to her husband. Part of being attractive is exhibiting the fruit of the Spirit. In order to do that, you must surrender your heart and soul to the Holy Spirit more and more. Every day you can say, "Lord, fill me afresh with the fruit of Your Spirit. Overflow me with Your love, joy, and peace. Teach me to be patient, kind, and good by growing in me Your longsuffering, kindness, and goodness. Help me to exhibit Your faithfulness, gentleness, and self-control" (Galatians 5:22-23).

This book will also help you truly understand that you belong to Jesus and that "those who are Christ's have crucified the flesh with its passions and desires" (Galatians 5:24). This doesn't mean you are passionless toward your husband. It means that the "I want what I want" in the way of expectations of him doesn't supersede the importance of "I want what *God* wants" in your attitude and mind. In order to want what God wants, you must walk in the Spirit (Galatians 5:25). When we live controlled by the flesh and not the Holy Spirit, nothing good comes of it. We end up thinking about ourselves and what *we* want and not what *God* wants. When we crucify our fleshly desires—and live in the Spirit so that we walk in the Spirit—we don't "become conceited, provoking one another, envying one another" (Galatians 5:26). We become more like the Lord instead. And that's what we all want.

These devotions and prayers will also help your husband to better hear from God, to increase his understanding of God's truth, to grow in strength and peace, and to gain proper perspective on various situations and challenges he may be facing. I have included many of the common attitudes and struggles found in most marriages. Each prayer for the two of you will help you both be more and more led by the Holy Spirit so that you can do what's right without allowing such things as negative reactions to each other get in the way.

One of the revelations I have personally received from the Lord in the last few years has been that I have a *choice* about my attitude and how I am going to react to my husband every day. Of course, I *knew* that, but knowing and doing are two different things. If I am irritated about something, I have to *decide* if I am going to act irritated when I talk to him for the next week. Or am I going to talk it out with him and choose to speak words that unite and not words that separate? Am I going to make sure that the first words I speak to him in the morning—or when I haven't seen him for a while—are pleasant and uplifting? These devotions and prayers help me make the right choice every day, and they will help you too.

If your husband is not yet a believer, I have not given you a separate prayer to pray in each devotion for him. That's because it is best to pray each day for his salvation. Say, "Lord, I pray You would open my husband's eyes to Your truth and lead him to salvation in You. Help him to know You, Jesus, and receive You as his Savior and Redeemer." Then pray the prayers in this book for him just as if he were already a believer, always thanking

God that He is leading your husband closer to salvation every day. The more you pray for your husband this way, the more his heart will become sensitive to the Holy Spirit's promptings. Even though he is not yet a believer, God can still speak to him. Your prayers can clear the air of worldly noise around his mind and heart so he can hear God better. Don't become discouraged and feel as though nothing is happening. If you are praying, then something is *definitely* happening. No matter how resistant your husband is to his own breakthrough, he is not too tough for God to break through to and save.

You can read this book straight through from beginning to end, or you can let the titles of each devotion lead you to the one that addresses what you are facing, experiencing, or needing right then. I pray you will meet the Lord in these Scriptures, devotions, and prayers in a new and powerful way, and see wonderful changes in you, your husband, and your marriage that only *He* can make.

Stormie Omartian

1

When I Desire Greater Persistence in Prayer

Rejoice always, pray without ceasing,
in everything give thanks;
for this is the will of God in
Christ Jesus for you.

1 THESSALONIANS 5:16-18

AS A WIFE, you need the kind of prayer habit that doesn't give up or allow discouragement to get in the way, but instead persists and keeps on praying and asking.

When God told Abraham He intended to determine if Sodom was deserving of destruction, Abraham then interceded, praying on behalf of however many righteous people might be there. He asked God if He would destroy Sodom if fifty righteous people were found there, and the Lord said He would not. Abraham then asked if He would destroy the city if forty-five righteous people were found there, then forty people, then thirty, then twenty. Each time Abraham asked, God said He would not destroy it for that many people. Finally Abraham said, "Suppose ten should be found there?" And God said, "I will not destroy it for the sake of ten" (Genesis 18:32). As it turned out, only four righteous people were there, so God destroyed it. But Abraham had stopped asking at ten.

We need the kind of persistence in prayer that causes us to continue asking as Abraham did. Too often we stop short. Perhaps Abraham stopped asking because he couldn't imagine that there wouldn't be at least ten righteous people in Sodom. Or perhaps by then God had proved His point and revealed His intentions. God knew the city was wicked enough to destroy, but He saved the four righteous people—which were Lot, his wife, and their two daughters (Genesis 19:29).

Your prayers are powerful to save too. So keep asking and continue seeking, and don't ask for crumbs when God wants to give you the banquet. When it comes to praying for you and your husband and your marriage, ask God to help you persist in prayer for even what may seem impossible. Ask for your marriage to not only be saved, but to be good. Ask for it to not only be good, but to be great. God doesn't say "No" to what is His will. If your husband has a strong will that refuses to submit to God's will, persist in praying that God's will wins out.

My Prayer to God

Lord, I pray You would help me to be persistent in prayer—to ask and keep asking for what I believe is Your will. I know anything less than love, selflessness, kindness, peace, and generosity of soul is not Your will in my relationship with my husband. Help me to persist in praying for nothing less than the high standard You have for our marriage. Give me a vision of how You want me to pray. Show me the way You want our marriage to be and help me to pray accordingly so that it becomes all that.

I know I cannot force my husband's will to be anything other than what it is, but You can touch his heart and turn it toward You. I pray You would do that. May he welcome Your Lordship in his life. Help me to pray consistently and passionately, and to persevere no matter what is happening. I thank You in advance for the great things You are going to do in both of us and in our marriage.

In Jesus' name I pray.

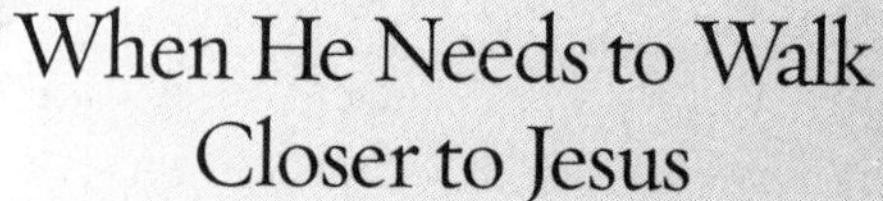

2

When He Needs to Walk Closer to Jesus

I am the vine, you are the branches.
He who abides in Me, and I in him,
bears much fruit; for without
Me you can do nothing.

JOHN 15:5

HAVE YOU EVER OBSERVED your husband becoming so busy or preoccupied that he seems to be drifting away from the things and ways of the Lord? It can easily happen to anyone if they are not careful to stay in God's Word and in constant communication with the Lord in prayer and worship. If you ever see this happening to your husband, pray for him to recognize that Jesus is the vine he must be plugged into or he will not bear fruit. Pray he will come to a clear understanding that he cannot accomplish anything lasting without Jesus in his life. Pray he recognizes that God wants to be glorified by the fruitfulness of his life (John 15:8). Pray the same thing for yourself as well. You need to be plugged into Jesus too so that you are living in Him and He is living in you. You cannot bear the fruit you want to see in your life if you don't have that deep abiding walk with Him every day and night.

If your husband does not yet have a walk with Jesus, continue to pray for that. Ask God to draw him closer to Himself, so that one day the Giver of fruitfulness will enable both of you to bear fruit together beyond what you ever dreamed possible. There isn't a husband on earth who couldn't benefit from his wife's prayers for him to have a closer walk with the Lord. And your happiness together will be greatly affected by it.

My Prayer to God

LORD, I pray my husband will be drawn into a closer walk with You. No matter how busy he becomes, I pray You will remind him that he cannot go off on his own without acknowledging You as the source of all that is good in his life. Give him the wisdom and discernment to see when he is becoming distracted by other things and neglecting his relationship with You. Give him a desire for more of You and Your Word. Enable him to see clearly that without You he can do nothing worthwhile or lasting. Give him a desire to plug into You in a deeper way, so that his connection with You produces great fruit in his life. Show me how to encourage and support him in that. Only You know what will speak to his heart.

I pray the same for me, that I will abide in You—my true vine—and You in me so that my life will bear much fruit in every way. Enable my husband and me to be fruitful together. Flow Your life through us in such a way that others see it and recognize You as the source of all that is good in our lives. May they know us by our fruit and praise You for it.

In Jesus' name I pray.

3

When We Must Work Together in Unity

Behold, how good and how pleasant it is
for brethren to dwell together in unity!

PSALM 133:1

AFTER THE FLOOD, Noah's descendents grew greatly in numbers, and they had only one language. They decided to build a city with a tower that would rise up to heaven. The Lord saw what they were doing and said, "Indeed *the people are one and they all have one language*, and this is what they begin to do; *now nothing that they propose to do will be withheld from them*" (Genesis 11:6, emphasis added). So God confused their language, scattered them over the earth, and caused them to stop building the city—which was called Babel.

From this story we can see the power of unity and speaking the same language. Because the people of Babel were in unity, they could accomplish anything they wanted to. But the negative consequences of their unity happened because they were not doing what *God* wanted them to do, and so He had to stop them. It's different in a marriage. Having unity is what keeps a marriage together, and that *is* what God wants. It is *His will* that you be in *unity* with your husband, and that you *speak the same language*, and *be on the same page*, for then you are fulfilling the purpose for which He joined you together.

Pray that you and your husband will be in unity with regard to your goals, attitudes, intentions, methods, and actions. Jesus said, "If two of you agree on earth concerning anything that they ask, it will be done for them by My Father in heaven" (Matthew 18:19). Pray you will agree on what you are praying about and wanting. When you do, you will see powerful answers to your prayers. Nothing will stand in your way when the two of you are united in God's purpose for your lives.

My Prayer to God

Lord, I pray You would help my husband and me to always be on the same page and speak the same language. When there are times we are not communicating well—where we seem to be missing each other's intentions, or we too often misunderstand each other's words—I pray Your perfect wisdom and knowledge would prevail between us. By the power of Your Spirit, I pray You would enable us to always have a clear understanding of each other and whatever situation we are in. Help us to resist the enemy—the author of confusion, lies, and deceit—and refuse to give place to any of his plans for our relationship as husband and wife. I pray that only You, Lord, will reign in our marriage, and that only Your Spirit of love and peace will rule between us.

You have said in Your Word that there isn't anything people cannot do when they are in unity (Genesis 11:6). I pray our unity means there is nothing we cannot do to make our marriage strong, and there is nothing the enemy can do to come between us. Enable us to pray together in unity so that we will see powerful answers to prayer, and that nothing of Your goodness and blessing will be withheld from our lives.

In Jesus' name I pray.

4

When I Need to Trust God in the Situation

Watch, stand fast in the faith,
be brave, be strong.
Let all that you do be done with love.

1 CORINTHIANS 16:13-14

WHEN SOMETHING SERIOUS HAPPENS in your marriage or your circumstances, you may worry and even become distraught with concern. Left uncontrolled, these concerns eat at you and your marriage relationship, and can destroy what you have built together. You must pray about them, of course, and preferably together, if your husband is willing. However, too often a man may be resistant to praying with his wife, either out of hard-heartedness or lack of belief in the power of God to answer prayer. But whether he prays with you or not, you still must give all your concerns to God.

When a grave situation occurs in your marriage, or something troubling happens to you or around you, and you don't see how it can ever be resolved, acknowledge before God that although you don't have the answers, you know *He* does. Tell Him how you feel and what you want Him to do. Ask Him to help you get to the point where you totally trust Him, knowing that even when you see no way out and no good solution, *He* can. You may feel hopeless about it, but in Him there is always hope. Ask Him to give you peace in the midst of this trial. Tell Him you look to Him and not the situation to determine your reaction to what has happened. Choose to trust the Lord's love and faithfulness toward you. Ask Him to do the impossible. He can and will.

My Prayer to God

LORD, I bring to You this seemingly impossible situation my husband and I are in. First of all, I want to confess any doubt in my heart that this will end well. I see no good way out without a miracle from You, but I don't want to carry negative thinking around with me, and so I release all doubt and fear into Your hands. I refuse to harbor unforgiveness toward my husband or anyone else whom I think may be responsible for this problem. I confess any unforgiveness I have before You, and I ask You to set me free of it. Help me to trust You to make this right.

Where either my husband or I have done something that has caused this, help us to learn from our mistakes. If we are in this dire situation due to no fault of our own, enable us to navigate these rough waters so that, although we may seem to be shipwrecked right now, we won't capsize and sink. Keep us from blaming each other and help us to look to You for a miracle rescue. Make us both strong in You as we face the future together.

Lord, I need Your peace, power, and love to reign in me. Increase my faith to trust You above all I see or feel. Help me to be watchful in prayer, and to stand fast in faith just as You have said to do in Your Word. Enable me to face these circumstances with courage and not defeat. I pray that everything I do and say, and the thoughts I think, will be motivated by Your love in my heart. I choose this day to trust You in the situation, asking that You would work a miracle of redemption in it.

In Jesus' name I pray.

5

When He Must Make the Right Decision

I will bless the Lord who has given me counsel;
my heart also instructs me in the night seasons.
I have set the Lord always before me;
because He is at my right hand I shall not be moved.

PSALM 16:7-8

SO MUCH OF THE QUALITY of your life as a wife depends on your husband making the right decisions. The consequences of his wrong decisions can greatly affect you and your children for a long time. But then, you are probably quite certain of that already.

The Bible says, "Every way of a man is right in his own eyes" (Proverbs 21:2). That means often something may seem like a good idea at the time, but it really isn't. That's why we must ask God about every decision we make. You may have worked hard all your life and saved and spent wisely, but if your husband is careless and makes a terrible business or financial decision, you can see all you have worked for go down the drain. That's why you must ask God to help not only *you*, but also your *husband* to make right decisions.

Any decision he makes—such as what job he takes, where to live, whom he spends time with, what he does for recreation, how he spends money, or how much time he spends with his family—will greatly affect your lives together. Hopefully, your husband will pray with you about any decisions he makes, but not all men are willing to do that. Many a man feels he should be able to make those decisions himself without any input from his wife or anyone else. I hope that is not your situation, but if it is, you can still ask God to keep him from making any mistakes. When your husband has a big decision to make, ask God to help him do the right thing. Of course, some men are so strong willed that they refuse to listen to the Holy Spirit speaking to their heart. But at least you prayed, and that leaves him in God's hands.

My Prayer to God

Lord, I pray You would help my husband make right decisions every day. Teach him to always discern Your will and to choose that over any desires of his flesh. Give him wisdom so that he won't make any terrible mistakes. Where he has made a wrong decision in the past and it has cost us dearly, I pray You would redeem that situation and bring restoration where it is needed. Only You can bring good out of disaster. You have said in Your Word that "there is a way that seems right to a man," but in the end it leads to death (Proverbs 14:12). Help my husband to discern between the way that *seems* right and the way that *is* right. Help him to distinguish the path that *leads to life* from the path that *leads to destruction.*

Whenever he has a decision to make, instruct him "in the night seasons" (Psalm 16:7). Speak to him in words he cannot ignore. Keep him from moving out on a path without clear knowledge of Your will. Help him to hear Your voice saying, "This is the way, walk in it" (Isaiah 30:21). Cause him to want us to pray together about important decisions so that we will always be in unity.

In Jesus' name I pray.

6

When We Need to Have Better Communication

Listen, for I will speak of excellent things,
and from the opening of my lips
will come right things.

PROVERBS 8:6

HOW MANY TIMES HAVE WE HEARD someone speak of their marriage relationship, saying the communication breakdown was so bad it had seriously hurt their ability to talk together at all? Have you ever thought or said something like that yourself? If you have never had communication problems in your marriage, you are greatly blessed and should thank God every day that you are married to someone who communicates openly with you. Pray it will always be that way.

One of the common problems in a marriage is miscommunication, which is different than no communication at all. At least there is an attempt to communicate. But when what is communicated is negative criticism, sarcasm, disrespect, or words that just came out wrong, then the problems between you begin to escalate. Enough poor or negative communication like that, along with the strife it brings, and eventually you stop talking because it is just not worth it. With some marriage partners there is no attempt to communicate. But unless something is wrong with a person mentally or physically, the reason for not communicating is usually selfishness—giving nothing—or extreme hurt, which means the person has been so emotionally injured in the past that they are afraid to open up to the possibility of being hurt again. It seems to them that it's better to not talk at all, but that makes life miserable and a marriage impossible.

Pray that God will help you and your husband communicate good and positive things clearly with each other. Whatever has happened in the past with regard to that, God can correct it. Communication is something He desires. And He wants you both to speak of "excellent things" (Proverbs 8:6). Communicate with God about communicating with your husband. The Lord is an expert on this subject, and He can teach you both to open up to Him first and then to each other. Ask the Lord to guide you so you have "right things" coming out of your mouth at all times and miscommunication doesn't happen.

My Prayer to God

LORD, I pray You would help my husband and me to communicate openly and honestly with each other about everything. I pray that wherever our communication with each other fails, You would restore it to what it should be. Teach us to take the time needed and not be so self-absorbed that we cannot talk in depth to each other. Destroy our selfishness and teach us to open up to each other. Help us refuse to shut off. If we have stopped talking because the relationship has been strife filled and there have been many hurts, I ask You to heal those old wounds and give us peace. Help us to break through all that and tear down any wall that has been erected between us.

You are the God of new beginnings, and so I pray You would help us to start over. Enable us to see each other in a fresh way so that we can talk to each other in a productive manner. Make us whole enough to be truthful and honest in a loving and kind way, and not have to hide our thoughts, feelings, and experiences. If there is anything hidden that needs to be exposed, I pray You would shine Your light on our deepest thoughts and preoccupations. Help us to honor each other by listening and responding. May we never be so preoccupied that we don't take time to communicate "right" and "excellent" things to each other.

In Jesus' name I pray.

7

When I Don't Feel Like Praying for Him

Moreover, as for me, far be it from me
that I should sin against the Lord
in ceasing to pray for you.

1 SAMUEL 12:23

THERE MAY BE DAYS when you just don't feel like praying for your husband. Probably nearly every woman has had them. You may be disappointed in him or angry at something he did or did not do. Whatever the reason, when that happens it's best to go before the Lord and pray for *you*. Don't worry about praying for him at this moment. *You* need prayer first. *You* obviously have need of more of the Lord's love, joy, peace, and comfort in your heart. And *you* must find release from your heavy burdens before you do anything else.

Bring all that is in your heart to the Lord. Perhaps there is deep hurt, sadness, anger, or discouragement you want to be free of right now. Maybe you have grown weary in well-doing. Go before God and tell Him what has happened and how you feel about it. He already knows, but He wants to hear it from you. That's because He desires that you draw close to Him, and more than anything else, that is the main reason He wants you to pray. It's your personal time in His presence.

Perhaps you have many challenges, and you've been praying and waiting for the answers, and you need God to redeem your soul "in peace from the battle" you are waging in prayer so you can rest (Psalm 55:18). Ask the Lord to give you renewal, rejuvenation, and revival in your heart and soul. Ask Him to show you the hope and power you have in Him. Don't worry about the concerns you have for your husband, your family, or anyone else right now. You are not sinning in ceasing to pray for your husband. You are taking a break to pray for yourself and be refreshed in the Lord. Every warrior needs a time to rest from the battle, and you are no different. You will pray for your husband again tomorrow. Rest in the Lord today.

My Prayer to God

Lord, I confess I don't feel like praying for my husband right now. I have thoughts and emotions that keep me from coming before You with a peaceful heart in that regard. I confess any anger, disappointment, or hurt I feel toward him. Reveal to me any other thoughts and feelings in me that are not glorifying to You so I can be free of them. Take away any hardness of my heart that has crept in and create in me a clean heart. Overflow me with Your love so that my heart can easily overflow with love to others.

I realize that more than anything else I need time with You to be refreshed and renewed. I lay down my battle in prayer for my husband, my marriage, my family, and the details of my life and release it all to You. I surrender every burden, concern, worry, desire, and hope to You and choose to simply be in Your presence. Rejuvenate my mind, fill my soul afresh with Your Spirit, teach me Your ways, and speak to me about my life in Christ. Comfort me as I take comfort in Your Word. Fill me with an abundance of Your love, peace, and joy. Restore me to full capacity so that I can serve You with unfailing strength.

In Jesus' name I pray.

8

When He Needs a Better Attitude

Cast away from you all the transgressions which you have committed, and get yourselves a new heart and a new spirit.

EZEKIEL 18:31

GOD GIVES US A CHOICE about what our attitude will be. We can *choose* to allow negativity to dominate our personality to the detriment of ourselves and all around us, or we can *choose* to be more like Christ. There are many factors that can affect this, such as stress, strife, financial pressure, traumatic events, mental strain, pain, or sickness. But no matter what is happening to us, we are still responsible for our attitude in the midst of it.

Your husband's attitude affects his health, your children, the atmosphere of your home, and his future, not to mention how it makes you feel. If he has allowed a bad attitude to become a way of life, it must be changed or it will wear you down and put tremendous strain on your marriage. A chronically negative attitude can make him sick in mind, soul, and body. He may not realize it, but he has a personal choice about what kind of attitude and spirit he maintains. He has to decide—especially when he is in the midst of difficult circumstances or troubling situations—what kind of man he is going to be. Your prayers can help him make the right choice.

If your husband too often has a bad or wrong attitude, you have to be strong in your refusal to be influenced by that. Don't allow him or anyone else to pull you into their negativity and bring you down. Carry that heavy burden to God in prayer instead. Pray for your husband to have a new heart and a new spirit. That's God's will for his life, and life is too short to settle for anything less.

My Prayer to God

LORD, I pray for my husband to be free of any negative attitude he has. Help him to see the good in his life and not the bad. I repent of any negativity I have had in my mind and have conveyed to my husband and children. I confess it as a lack of faith in Your goodness in my life. I know that negativity doesn't do anyone any good. It is in itself a statement of faithlessness and self-centered sin. Please redeem any damage I may have done to my husband's soul by allowing any negative attitude to have a safe harbor in me. I also confess any lack of patience I may have had with his less than uplifting attitude. Forgive me and renew a right spirit within me.

I pray You will give my husband "a new heart and a new

spirit." Fill him with Your peace so that it dominates his personality. Let Your spirit of joy rise in him, no matter what his circumstances are right now. Teach him to refuse "sorrow of the heart" that breaks one's spirit (Proverbs 15:13). Strengthen and teach him to reject negativity and choose to have the "continual feast" of a merry heart (Proverbs 15:15). Help him to choose an attitude of love, patience, and kindness that comes only from inviting Your Holy Spirit to crowd out any other spirit that is trying to oppress him. Enable him to choose a spirit of praise and thankfulness to rule in his heart and mind.

In Jesus' name I pray.

9

When We Must Break Our Silence

Unless the Lord had been my help,
my soul would soon have settled in silence.

PSALM 94:17

THIS VERSE HAS TO DO WITH standing up for what's right and not staying silent, thereby allowing something unjust to happen. There are times in your marriage when you cannot settle for silence, either. When a husband and wife let silence continue, they are allowing a gap to grow between them that will widen into a gulf. For example, there can be occasions in a marriage relationship when *not* talking for a time is safer and more pleasant than talking, because speaking to each other about anything could trigger an argument. And so it becomes just not worth it to even speak. The problem with that is even though not speaking can be a temporary fix while tempers cool, this silent separation can grow into something bigger and more damaging if allowed to go on too long.

These self-initiated silences can also happen because one person is trying to protect himself or herself from an aggressor. ("If I don't say anything, then I won't trigger a rampage.") Or it could be because of selfishness. ("If I can't win this argument, then I won't say anything because I know I'm right.") Or immaturity. ("I'm going to punish her by not speaking to her.") Whatever the reason, continued silence is not of the Lord.

If you ever find the grip of silence closing in on you and your husband, pray immediately that God will help each of you to break it. If just one person is determined not to speak to the other, pray that God will bring down that prison of human will. And it truly can become a prison, the oppression of which you can feel every moment you are held captive by it. Pray for a dissolving of that silence with the steel-melting presence of the Holy Spirit's fire. He can melt down any wall—even that of a silent partner.

My Prayer to God

LORD, whenever there is deliberate and lasting silence between my husband and me, and it is raising a wall between us and causing a separation of hearts, I pray You would smash it down. I know it does not line up with Your view of us as being one. Soften any hardness of our hearts and heal the hurts that cause us to withdraw from each other for self-protection. Take away any attempts to punish through silence. Help us to rise above our own selfishness. Cause us to be so full of Your Spirit instead of ourselves that we forget we have silently agreed to not speak.

I also pray that when either of us has decided to withhold communication—where even though we have not stopped speaking completely, we still only communicate the absolute minimum in order to get along—keep us from being willing to settle for this deplorable lack of compassion and love. Help us to trust each other enough to share our thoughts and feelings in a calm and hopeful manner. Where one of us is volatile and can be easily set off, I pray You would squelch that rebellious spirit and convict the soul that gives it a safe harbor. Dissolve any silent divide between us and fill us both with Your Spirit of love, peace, and unity.

In Jesus' name I pray.

10

When I Have to Rise Above the Things That Irritate Me

May the God of patience and
comfort grant you to be
like-minded toward one another,
according to Christ Jesus,
that you may with one mind and one mouth
glorify the God and Father of our Lord Jesus Christ.

ROMANS 15:5-6

EVEN THE MOST PERFECT OF PEOPLE can irritate you sometimes. The greatest of houseguests can stay too long. The best of friends can be too frank. But when your husband repeatedly does something that irritates you, it can become unbearable. We all do things that would be annoying to some people if they were around us all the time. Because a husband and wife live so closely together, they each have the potential to irritate each other. That's why this is a matter worth committing to prayer.

If your husband does anything that irritates you, ask God to give you an abundance of patience and help you rise above it. I know this can seem very petty, but a small irritation can become a major issue after a while. The Bible says that it is our glory "to overlook a transgression" (Proverbs 19:11). It works to our benefit when we do. But sometimes, after years of overlooking the same transgression, we don't have it in ourselves to overlook it anymore. We need the power of God enabling us to do so. It's part of becoming like-minded and living in unity.

If you are at the point where your husband is doing something you cannot bear to live with for the rest of your life, ask the God of peace to prepare the way in both of your hearts to talk it out. Don't live constantly irritated. Ask God to help you let go of things that don't matter, but work together with your husband on the things that do. Pray that God will show you anything *you* do that irritates your husband. There is a way for two people to live in peace and satisfaction, and you must ask God to help you find it.

My Prayer to God

LORD, I bring to You the things that irritate me about my husband. I know there must be things I do to irritate him as well, so I pray You would help us both to be more considerate of each other. Neither of us wants to become critical and petty, but we need Your help in order to work this out. Enable us to become like-minded toward each other according to Your Word. Where either of us has irritating habits that need to be broken, help us to become free of them. Help me to overlook his faults, and help him to overlook mine.

Give me greater patience and tolerance and the kind

of peace in my heart that allows inconsequential things to roll off my back. At the same time, teach me to address in love the things that need to be confronted. I don't want to be a wife who seethes in silence, building up like a pressure cooker ready to explode. Take away all pent-up emotions in me and evaporate any critical attitude I have acquired because of them. Help me to not continue on another moment with irritation in my heart, but rather to submit everything to You for Your correction. Lift me above the things that could bring us both down. Enable us to learn to live together in total peace.

In Jesus' name I pray.

11

When He Needs to Understand the Power of His Own Words

Death and life are in the power of the tongue, and those who love it will eat its fruit.

PROVERBS 18:21

MANY MEN DON'T FULLY COMPREHEND the power and impact of their words. Just by reason of being male, a man's voice has the strength to be intimidating. A man can say something casually, carelessly, or insensitively without even realizing that he has frightened or hurt someone. Not all men use their voice to that degree, but many do. A man has the power to heal or harm the heart of those to whom he speaks, and never is that more true than within his marriage and family.

What your husband says to you or your children—and the way he says it—can build up or tear down. His words can strengthen family relationships or break them apart. You cannot have a successful and fulfilling marriage when your husband is careless or thoughtless in the words he speaks or the manner in which he speaks them. When a husband speaks hurtful words to his wife, he strikes her soul with a damaging blow far greater than he may realize. If your husband ever does that, pray he will understand his potential to intimidate or even wound.

Ask God to help your husband hear what he is saying and the way he says it even *before* he says it. The book of Proverbs says, "He who guards his mouth preserves his life, but he who opens wide his lips shall have destruction" (13:3). Pray that God will fill your husband's heart with an abundance of His love, patience, kindness, and goodness so that they overflow in the words he speaks to you and your children. If your husband has never hurt another with his words, then thank God for that and pray he never will. Pray that his gentle spirit will rub off on the other men around him.

My Prayer to God

Lord, I pray You would lead my husband in the way he speaks to me and our family. Help him to build up with his words and not tear down. Teach him to bless and not curse, to encourage and not discourage, to inspire and not intimidate. I pray when he must speak words that are hard for others to hear, help him speak them from a kind heart. Your Word says that out of the overflow of our hearts we speak (Matthew 12:34). If ever his heart is filled with anger, resentment, or selfishness, I pray he will see that as sin and repent of it. Fill him instead with an abundance of Your love, peace, and joy. Help him to understand that "life and death are in the power of the tongue" and there are consequences to the words he says (Proverbs 18:21).

Where my husband has been abusive or hurtful in the words he has spoken to me, I pray You would convict his conscience about that and cause him to see the damage he is doing to me and to our marriage. If I have spoken words to him that have caused harm to our relationship, forgive me. Enable me to speak words that will bring healing. Help us both to think carefully about what we say to each other and to our children and how we say it (Proverbs 15:28). Enable us to always consider the consequences of the words we speak. I know we have a choice about what we say and the way we say it. Help us both to always make the right choice.

In Jesus' name I pray.

12

When We Want to See Answers to Our Prayers

If you abide in Me, and My words abide in you,
you will ask what you desire, and
it shall be done for you.

John 15:7

We all desperately need answers to our prayers—especially when we are married. It's hard to imagine how people maintain a successful marriage without help from God. But we don't automatically receive answers to our prayers just because we prayed them. God doesn't say, "Ask Me for anything and I'll see that you get it." He says, "Walk with Me and let My Word live in you, and *then* ask." In other words, we have to live God's way, spend time with Him, and read His Word so often that it is alive in us. When we do that, *then* we can ask what we desire and it will be done.

Walking with God and living in His Word changes your heart and causes you to become more like Him. That means what you will be asking for in prayer is going to be more in line with God's will.

The way to see answers to your prayers is to first ask God to deepen both your husband's and your own relationship with Him. Ask God to grow His Word daily in both of you. Pray that the desires of your heart line up with the desires of *God's*, and pray the same for your husband. Then you will be living according to God's ways, and you will have aligned yourself with the flow of God's blessings in answer to prayer.

My Prayer to God

LORD, my husband and I long to see answers to our prayers. We cannot live successfully without You working powerfully in our lives, but I know that answers to our prayers come only as we walk with You and let Your Word live in us. I pray You would draw my husband and me so close to You that we will not take a step without Your guidance. Help us to truly abide in Your presence day by day. Enable us to understand Your Word and be transformed by it as we read it and learn it. Weave it in our hearts so that it becomes part of the fabric of our lives that grows stronger every day.

Enable my husband and me to pray according to Your will, so that the desires of our hearts line up with the desires of Yours. Lord, You know how much we need to see answers to our prayers, so I pray You will help us do all that is necessary to keep our prayers from being hindered in any way. Teach us to pray in power so that we will see powerful answers. Help us to frequently pray together, as well as alone. Above all, we want Your will to be done in our lives, so guide us to pray accordingly, trusting that Your answers will be for our greatest good. We praise You and thank You in advance for hearing our prayers and for answering them in Your way and Your time.

In Jesus' name I pray.

13

When I Have to Confess Something to My Husband

Confess your trespasses to one another,
and pray for one another, that you may be healed.
The effective, fervent prayer of a
righteous man avails much.

JAMES 5:16

THERE ARE TIMES in every wife's life when she needs to confess something to her husband that will be hard for him to hear. For example, if she has dented the car, or spent too much money, or overdrawn the bank account, or accidentally given away his favorite football shirt—or something even worse—and she knows his reaction to what she has to tell him will not be good, she needs help from above. If this happens to you, the thing to do is pray *before* you speak.

If you have something to tell your husband you know he will not approve of, ask God to help you break it to him in the best way possible. Don't just blurt it out. Ask God to prepare your husband's heart to hear hard things without having a bad reaction to them. Ask the Lord to give you the right words to say and the right time to say it. There may be occasions when your husband needs to confess something to you, and you will want to set a good example of calm and patience for him to want to emulate.

If you feel your husband overreacts to things, pray that God will give him a compassionate and understanding heart and an even temper. Ask God to plant in him the desire to pray for you instead of criticize or lecture. After you seek your husband's forgiveness, tell him how effective it would be to pray together about this so that it never happens again.

My Prayer to God

Lord, help me to speak to my husband about what I know I need to confess to him. Give me the words to say. Open his heart to receive what I need to tell him with a good and godly attitude. If it is something I know I did wrong, help me to not do it again. Give me the wisdom and discernment I need to avoid that in the future. Where it is something I did that I feel was *not* wrong, but I know he will not be happy about it, help us to talk calmly and peacefully about this issue. Enable us to come to an agreement regarding what should be done in the future.

Give my husband and me compassionate attitudes that don't resort to anger. Help us to talk peacefully and come to a mutual understanding so that we always exhibit respect for each other. Teach us to believe for the best in each other. When I have to confess something that is hard for him to hear, reign in both of our hearts so that our words glorify You. Where there are things that should be confessed to each other but have been hidden because of not wanting to stir up anything negative, I pray You would help us to get these things out in the open honestly. Your Word says that confessing our trespasses—both to You and to each other—can be a prelude to healing, not only of body and soul but also of our relationship and marriage. Enable us to freely confess and freely pray for each other so that we may find the healing we need.

In Jesus' name I pray.

14

When He Must Hear What I Have to Tell Him

Let every man be swift to hear,
slow to speak, slow to wrath;
for the wrath of man does not produce
the righteousness of God.

JAMES 1:19-20

OFTEN WE WIVES are tuned in to things our husbands are not. There are times when you see the truth about a situation and your husband doesn't, and you know he needs to hear your input. For example, if you see your husband about to go over a cliff by making a wrong decision, you must absolutely say something to him. If there are words you need to speak to your husband with regard to what he is doing or not doing, *pray first*. Ask God to open his ears to hear, his mind to understand, and his heart to receive what you have to say.

There is a type of man who refuses to listen to anything his wife says simply because she is a woman and he is convinced he knows better. Sometimes it hurts his ego to think she could be right and he might be wrong. Most men, however, have a healthy self-image and know it doesn't minimize them to receive input from their wife. In fact, they welcome it.

When Sarah realized something was happening in her family that wasn't right, she knew she had to speak. When she told Abraham about it, what she said was something Abraham did not want to hear. He rejected the idea at first, but then God told him, "Do not let it be displeasing in your sight...whatever Sarah has said to you, listen to her voice..." (see Genesis 21:9-12). Don't you love that? God told Abraham to listen to his wife because she was right. Pray that God will help your husband see when you are right as well. Ask God to open your husband's heart to hear from *Him*, even as you are speaking.

My Prayer to God

LORD, I pray You will show me the truth about what I need to see regarding my husband. Help me to know if whatever I am sensing in my soul about him or his situation is really a revelation from You. If I am wrong, show me what is right. If I am right about this, prepare my husband's heart to receive what I have to say to him. Open his ears to hear the truth and keep him from being resistant or defensive. Help me to speak to him with the patience, kindness, humility, and self-control that come from walking with You and being filled with Your Spirit.

Sarah knew what was right, yet when she told Abraham about it he wasn't in agreement with her. But You spoke to him, and he heard Your voice and saw the truth. I pray that whenever I must speak to my husband about a situation I am seeing in my spirit, You will speak the truth to him that he needs to hear. I am not concerned about whether he thinks I am right, but more concerned that he understands Your will for his life and our lives together, and that he does the right thing. Help my husband to be swift to hear Your voice, and slow to say no before he has even heard the matter through. Prepare his heart now and give me the words I need to say. If I should not say anything at all, show me that too.

In Jesus' name I pray.

15

When We Need to Talk Things Out

He who answers a matter before he hears it,
it is folly and shame to him.

PROVERBS 18:13

HAVE YOU EVER EXPRESSED a concern or thought to your husband but didn't feel he really heard you? Does he sometimes not give as much weight to what you are saying as you think the matter deserves? Have there been times when you tried to talk to your husband, but you felt as if he answered or commented too quickly without waiting to really hear you out?

Being able to talk things through is an important issue, but it is impossible to do that effectively without each person taking time to really hear what the other one has to say.

If your husband is a talker and not a listener, you may feel that he doesn't *want* to listen to you or doesn't value what you have to say. And if *you* are a talker and not a listener, he may feel the same way about you. Whoever it is that constantly wants to rush through a conversation in order to get on to "more important" things is doing damage to the relationship.

Talking things out is a huge building block in a marriage. When that seldom happens, gaping holes are left in the relationship, and you end up building on a shaky foundation. Ask God to help you and your husband talk things out in a friendly and noncombative manner. Ask for a spirit of clarity, patience, peace, and love to reign between you. Pray that God will give you ears to hear each other every day. Ask Him to help you both talk about important things until they are resolved so they are not just left on the back burner to turn into a blazing and destructive fire later on.

My Prayer to God

Lord, I pray You would help my husband and me to calmly and maturely talk things out without any arguments, strife, misunderstanding, or oversensitivity. Enable us to clearly share our perspectives on the issues at hand and truly listen to and hear each other. Give us Your peace and patience and the ability to share our opinions without attacking each other in any way. Show us how to resolve conflict when it arises so that any issue needing to be resolved will be mutually decided upon in a mature way. Put an end to any heated discourse that ignites overly strong feelings in either of us. Instead, help us to understand and fully believe without reservation that we are on the same team and we should always be working to keep the teamwork strong.

Whenever the enemy attempts to get in between us and

cause confusion, misunderstanding, oversensitivity, feelings of rejection, or the *fear* of rejection, help us to discern the source and refuse his influence in our lives. Enable us to thoroughly talk out every issue so it is completely dealt with and there are no loose ends dangling without resolution. Help us to do all this with a positive, loving, and compassionate attitude toward each other.

In Jesus' name I pray.

16

When I Want to Be More Like Jesus

Whoever keeps His word, truly the love of God is perfected in him. By this we know that we are in Him. He who says he abides in Him ought himself also to walk just as He walked.

1 John 2:5-6

NOTHING REVEALS to a woman how close or far away she is from being like Jesus than the relationship she has with her husband. The way she thinks, talks, acts, and *reacts* around him—or in *response* to him—shows her how far she has to go in order to become all that God wants her to be.

Marriage is one of the true testing grounds for what is in all of us. Any selfishness, inconsideration, or lack of love in either a husband or wife will be revealed as they live together day after day, year after year. But if ever a woman doesn't like what she sees happening in herself with regard to her marriage relationship, she can seek to be more like Jesus, so that His love, selflessness, and kindness will grow in her and be revealed to those around her—especially her husband. (A man can and should do the same thing, of course, but this is about you right now.)

Ask God to help you walk as Jesus walked. The only way to actually do that is by the power of the Holy Spirit. If you have received Jesus, then you have His Holy Spirit in you, and you can live God's way because the Holy Spirit enables you to do so. The way to have the perfect love of Jesus grow in you is to *be daily in God's Word* so you can hear from Him about how to live, and you can read about the way Jesus lived, and you can *let the Word live in you* so you can be led by God's Spirit to make the right choices about how to live your life. The Bible says if we say we know God and do not keep His commandments, we have no truth in us (1 John 2:4). Thank God that you have the mind of Christ and therefore all you need to become more Christlike. Ask the Holy Spirit to lead you and teach you and enable you to have the same compassion, selflessness, forgiveness, mercy, and love toward your husband that Jesus has toward you. Ask Him to fill you with His truth.

My Prayer to God

LORD, help me to think like You, act like You, and talk like You—with compassion, love, grace, and mercy. Take away everything in me that is not of You—all anger, bitterness, criticism, and lack of love. Remove every tendency in me to function in the flesh and lash out with my words or actions. Take away any desire in me to withdraw from my husband, whether physically, emotionally, or mentally. I know that holding myself apart from him is not what You want me to do, for Your nature is to have us draw close to each other as You draw close to us, and I want to imitate You.

Lead me in Your ways, Lord. Teach me what Your unconditional love means and help me to display it. Fill me so full of Your love and forgiveness that it overflows from me to my husband. Mold my heart into the way You want it to be. Change me every time I read Your Word. Help me to be so sold out to You that I cannot move or speak apart from the love You put in my heart. Lord, You are beautiful, kind, gentle, faithful, true, unselfish, wise, lovely, peaceful, good, and holy. You are light and life. Enable me to be more like You.

In Jesus' name I pray.

17

When He Must Say He's Sorry

He who covers his sins will not prosper,
but whoever confesses and forsakes
them will have mercy.

PROVERBS 28:13

IF YOUR HUSBAND HURTS YOU in some way—whether intentionally, carelessly, or unknowingly—you want him to recognize what happened, confess his mistake, and say he is sorry. Of course, you can't *make* him *feel* sorry, but you can pray that God will convict his heart about it and lead him to confess that he is sorry to you.

The reason to pray that your husband apologizes for whatever he has said or done is not to see him crawl. And it is not only to find healing for the hurt, as important as that is for you. It's because when he doesn't repent of what he has done it means he is covering up his sin, and that limits his ability to prosper. And the two of you cannot live successfully without God's blessing of prosperity upon you.

You don't want your husband doing something—or *not* doing something—that separates him from the Lord in any way. Your prayers for him can help him to see the truth more clearly, because the Spirit of truth will convict his heart. Also, your prayers can help him to be confident enough to recognize that his apology to you will *raise* your esteem for him and not lower it. Although it is hard for a less confident person to admit when he is wrong, a husband who feels better about himself is more likely to see the benefit of clearing the air between you. And that always makes for a better marriage relationship.

My Prayer to God

Lord, if there is an offense my husband has committed against me, or a way in which he has neglected me, and he should say he is sorry, I pray You will help him to do so. Draw him close to You so that he can confess any sins he has committed to You. Help him to clear the air with You first so that he will feel greater clarity and confidence in his ability to clear the air with me. You have said in Your Word that if we come to worship You and remember that someone has something against us because of an offense we have committed, we are to go first to find that person and apologize, and then bring our worship to You (Matthew 5:23-24). Convict my husband's heart about that so nothing interferes with his relationship with You.

Prepare my heart with forgiveness now so that I will receive his apology with a right attitude. Take away anything in me that wants him to feel bad for the offense he has committed. Remove all desire in me to punish. When he *does* say he is sorry to me, I pray that this will be the end of the matter and we don't have to revisit it again. Help us both to let go of all offenses and be able to move forward to better things. Above all, I want him to know Your mercy and be able to prosper in every way.

In Jesus' name I pray.

18

When We Want God to Breathe New Life into Our Marriage

Do not remember the former things,
nor consider the things of old.
Behold, I will do a new thing, now it
shall spring forth; shall you not know it?
I will even make a road in the wilderness
and rivers in the desert.

ISAIAH 43:18-19

WE ALL HAVE TIMES when we know we need new life in our marriage. We feel the strain, the tension, the sameness, or possibly even the subtle decay in it. When there is so much water under the bridge over what seems like a river of hurt, apathy, or preoccupation, we know we cannot survive the slowly and steadily rising flood without the Lord doing a new thing in both of us. The good news is that God says He will do that. He is the God of new beginnings, after all. But it won't happen if we don't make a choice to let go of the past.

We have been made new if we have received Jesus. "If anyone is in Christ, he is a new creation; old things have passed away; behold, all things have become new" (2 Corinthians 5:17). But in a marriage, it is way too easy to hang on to the old disappointments, misunderstandings, disagreements, and abuses. It becomes a wilderness of hurtful memories we cling to because we don't want to be hurt, disappointed, misunderstood, disregarded, fought with, or abused again.

Hanging on to old patterns of thought and negative memories keeps them fresh in your mind. And you don't let your husband forget them, either. You remain mired in them because you don't feel the situation has been resolved—and it still hurts. Only God can give you and your husband a new beginning from all that has gone on in the past. Only He can make a road in the wilderness of miscommunication and misread intentions, and make a *cleansing* and *restoring* river to flow in the dry areas of your relationship. Everyone needs new life in their marriage at certain times. And only the God of renewal can accomplish that.

My Prayer to God

LORD, I ask that You would do a fresh work of Your Spirit in our marriage. Make all things new in each of us individually and also together. Dissolve the pain of the past where it is still rising up in us to stifle our communication and ultimately our hope and joy. Wherever we have felt trapped in a wilderness of our own making, carve a way out of it for us and show us the path to follow. If there are rigid and dry areas between us that don't allow for new growth, give us a fresh flow of Your Spirit to bring new vitality into our relationship. Help us to stop rehearsing old hurtful conversations that have no place in any life committed to the God of new beginnings. Sweep away all the old rubble of selfishness, stubbornness, blindness, and the inability to see beyond the moment or a particular situation.

Only You can take away our painful memories so that we don't keep reliving the same problems, hurts, or injustices. Only You can resurrect love, excitement, and hope where they have died. Help us to forgive fully and allow each other to completely forget. Help us to focus on Your greatness in us, instead of each other's faults. Holy Spirit, breathe new life into each of us and into our marriage today.

In Jesus' name I pray.

19

When I Am Disappointed in Him

He will fulfill the desire of those who fear Him;
He also will hear their cry and save them.

PSALM 145:19

WHEN YOUR HUSBAND has done something to hurt, embarrass, or betray you, you may be disappointed in him for a legitimate reason. But God is all about love and forgiveness. He gives you the responsibility of making certain that you forgive fully and retain your love and respect for your husband. That can be very hard to do—especially if the offense has been repeated again and again. Or if the offense is quite serious. The truth is, you cannot come up with the kind of forgiveness needed without the help of God. That means you must pray for it.

First of all, go before the Lord and confess your disappointment and hurt to Him. Ask Him to heal your heart and work complete forgiveness in it for your husband. That is probably the last thing you feel like doing if the offense has been devastating, but for your own good and the good of your marriage, you must do it and quickly. Unforgiveness destroys you when you don't act right away to get rid of it. Forgiving is God's way, and His ways are for your benefit.

Be honest with God and tell Him how you feel and why. He already knows, but He wants to hear it from you. Be perfectly honest with your husband too. He needs to understand how what he has done has affected you. Forgiving him is not letting him off the hook. It's not saying that what he did is now fine with you. It's releasing him to God and letting the Lord deal with what he has done. Ask God to work complete forgiveness in you and take away all disappointment so that none remains in your heart. That can sometimes take a miracle, but God is the expert in that.

My Prayer to God

Lord, I confess any disappointment I have in my heart for my husband. I bring all the hurt and unforgiveness I feel to You and ask You to wash me clean of it. Fill my heart with an abundance of Your love and forgiveness. Convict both me and my husband if we have strayed from Your ways in response to one another. Show us where we are wrong. If he has done wrong, convict his heart about it. If I have overreacted to him, show me that too. When he says or does anything that is hurtful to me—that I feel disrespects me—show him the truth and help him to see it. If I do anything that disappoints or disrespects him, open my eyes and heart to understand what I should do differently.

I pray for an end to all hurtful words and actions between us. Teach me to respond the way You would have me to. Help me to speak only words to him that are pleasing to You. Heal my heart and his as well. Help us to overcome any and all disappointments successfully. Thank You that You hear my prayers and will fulfill my desire for a relationship with my husband that is free of personal disappointments and unfair judgments. Give us hearts of praise to You for all that we are grateful for in each other.

In Jesus' name I pray.

20

When He Needs Direction

A man's heart plans his way, but the Lord directs his steps.

PROVERBS 16:9

WE ALL NEED DIRECTION from the Lord. In our culture today we encounter so much deception, and without the Holy Spirit leading us we will have a hard time distinguishing the truth from a lie. And how can we make sound decisions without His wisdom? The Holy Spirit is our guide in all things, and it is He who gives wisdom, knowledge, and revelation. "When He, the Spirit of truth, has come, He will guide you into all truth; for He will not speak on His own authority, but whatever He hears He will speak; and He will tell you things to come" (John 16:13).

We can make all the plans we want, and we do need to do that, but ultimately it will still be the direction of the Holy Spirit that will direct us on the right path. He will usher us into all that is right and true for our lives.

Your husband needs knowledge and guidance from the Lord every day, and you can pray that he will have it. Pray he will clearly hear the voice of God speaking to him above all voices—even those of well-meaning people, or those who want to influence him for their own gain, or the voice of the enemy trying to take him off the path God has for him. Pray the same for yourself every time you ask God for direction on behalf of your husband. The Holy Spirit is the only true guide into all that is right for his life, your life, and your lives together.

My Prayer to God

LORD, I pray You would guide my husband through this day and in every decision he must make. Enable him to always discern the truth from a lie. Keep him from becoming blinded by deception and led down the wrong path. Teach him to search Your Word so that the truth is in his heart. Give him a fresh flow of Your wisdom. Put in him a holy barometer that has a deception meter ringing loudly in his mind and heart whenever he is about to be swayed away from Your best for his life. Lead him far from all that is not Your will. Enable him to hear Your voice instructing him in the way he should go. Keep him from being influenced by wrong voices who don't have his best interests at heart. Enable him to hear Your voice above all, telling him the right thing to do.

I pray You would guide me as well. Help me to hear Your voice in every decision either of us must make so that I can be a help and support to him. Give him the desire to pray with me about decisions that must be made. Only You, Lord, know what is best for him, and for me, and for us together. And only Your Holy Spirit can guide us in all truth. Enable both of us to know Your truth in our hearts at all times.

In Jesus' name I pray.

21

When We Want the Kind of Love That Pleases God

Love suffers long and is kind;
love does not envy; love does not parade itself,
is not puffed up; does not behave rudely,
does not seek its own,
is not provoked, thinks no evil;
does not rejoice in iniquity,
but rejoices in the truth; bears all things,
believes all things,
hopes all things, endures all things.
Love never fails.

1 CORINTHIANS 13:4-8

GOD MAKES IT CRYSTAL CLEAR in His Word about the kind of love He wants us to have. Sometimes we may wish it weren't so clear, because what is *also* clear is that we can't express this kind of love on a consistent basis without His help. He wants us to have love that is shown in patience and kindness and is not possessive. Love that is not arrogant, rude, demanding, or selfish. Love that does not become irritable or grumpy, and does not keep a list of injustices. Love that believes for the best in others and not the worst, and is happy for their success and not their failure. Love that never gives up on the other person and endures through whatever happens.

God not only wants you to have that kind of love for others, but He also wants you to have it for your husband. And He wants your husband to always exhibit that kind of love for you.

How in the world do you find love within you like that? Do you have the kind of love in your heart that is never selfish or impatient? Do you have the kind of love that can endure anything and never doubt or lose hope? Only the love of God *in* you can accomplish all that *through* you. The way you access the flow of God's love is by being in His presence—in prayer, praise, and worship. It comes by inviting the Holy Spirit to fill you afresh each day with *His* love and allowing His love to transform you.

My Prayer to God

Lord, I pray You would pour Your amazing, unconditional love into my heart and into my husband's heart as well. Help us to love each other the way You love us. I know we don't have it in us to do that on our own, but I also know Your Holy Spirit can fill us with Your love so that it overflows to each other. Enable us to have the kind of love that shows patience with each other, love that is kind and does good, love that doesn't become possessive or jealous, love that is not arrogant and always trying to steal attention away from the other, love that is never rude or selfish, love that is not hostile or easily irritable, love that believes for the best and not the worst in each other, love that is not resentful and doesn't keep a record of every offense, love that stands strong no matter what happens and doesn't lose hope and faith, love that never gives up. Enable us to have love for each other that will not fail.

Lord, You know what we are made of and how imperfect we are. We recognize we can't begin to do this without Your working a miracle in our hearts. I ask for a continual flow of Your presence and love in our lives today and every day. Help us to have the kind of love for each other that pleases You.

In Jesus' name I pray.

22

When I Need to Be Delivered from Bad Habits

For what I am doing, I do not understand.
For what I will to do, that I do not practice;
but what I hate, that I do…
But now, it is no longer I who do it,
but sin that dwells in me.

ROMANS 7:15,17

AT ONE TIME OR ANOTHER in our lives, we women struggle with some kind of habit or behavior we don't like, don't want, and don't know how to overcome. We usually know when we are doing something that is not good for our body, health, finances, or marriage, because after we do it we feel guilty to the point of self-flagellating regret. We beat ourselves up all day long about it.

In the verses above, Paul describes our situation when we *don't do* the things we know we should, and we *do* the things we know we shouldn't. It happens when sin gets control over us, or our flesh cries loudly for what it wants, or the enemy takes advantage of our weakness and we don't resist him. If we attempt to handle this on our own without God's help, even if we do well for a time, we may eventually fall back into the same bad habit. Paul, however, gives us reason to hope, because a few verses later he asks, "Who will deliver me from this?" And he answers his own question saying, "Jesus Christ our Lord" (Romans 7:24-25). Jesus can set us free from all that is destructive in our lives, including our tendency toward any bad habits.

The best news is that even though our own strength fails, the power of the Holy Spirit in us never fails. Ask God to set you free from any bad habit or craving that you know is not God's will for your life. Thank Him that because of Jesus, you don't have to give in to the dictates of your own flesh. Jesus has not only set you free, He can also help you walk in the freedom He has given you.

My Prayer to God

LORD, I pray You would expose any bad habits I have to Your light. Burn them out of my life. For the habit I struggle with most that I would like to see broken, help me to gain control over it so it cannot control me anymore. Show me how to rise up in the power of Your Spirit and resist this weakness head on. Take away whatever is in me that draws me to do anything that is not Your best for my life. Fill what is missing in me with more of You so that I stop trying to fill any empty place in my life with something that turns into an undesirable habit.

Destroy the conflict in me that causes me to do what I

don't want to do and *not* do what I *do* want to do. Enable me to be strong and not give in to weakness. I release to You all my desires and needs, and recognize that my true need will always be for more of You. Thank You, Jesus, for setting me free from captivity to sin and delivering me from all that is not good for me, and therefore not good for my husband and children. Protect me from anything that would drive me back into old habits that only destroy my peace, health, security, and future. Lift me above my weaknesses so that Your strength will be clearly manifested in me.

In Jesus' name I pray.

23

When He Carries a Heavy Burden

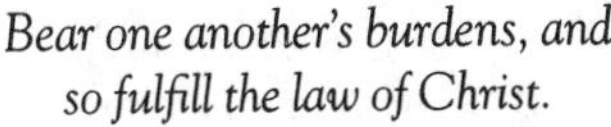

Bear one another's burdens, and so fulfill the law of Christ.

GALATIANS 6:2

SOCIETY PUTS A LOT OF WEIGHT on a man's shoulders. It is his burden to earn the finances to support his family. He is expected to do well at his work and on his job. There are so many expectations of him in that regard that he *feels* the pressure of it constantly. That's why you read about so many men committing suicide when they are in serious financial trouble. The burden is too great. Few women commit suicide for financial failure. If you or I fell into financial ruin, we would just sell everything, pay off all the debts we could, get a job, and start over. Men can feel the burden of failure in life-threatening ways. That's why your husband needs your prayers to keep his burdens lifted.

One of the best ways to bear your husband's burden is to pray for him about whatever heavy load he is carrying. Every time you do, pray especially for what burdens him the most. One of the most effective things you can do is let him know you are praying for him and ask him to tell you what his burdens are. He may reveal something you didn't even know was bothering him.

God's Word says that sometimes our burden comes from the oppressor. The children of Israel had an oppressor, and they were overtaken by this oppressor because of their own disobedience. But God promised that the burden the oppressor put on them would eventually be broken by the power of His Spirit. "It shall come to pass in that day that his burden will be taken away from your shoulder, and his yoke from your neck, and the yoke will be destroyed because of the anointing oil" (Isaiah 10:27). The anointing oil refers to a work of the Holy Spirit. Your prayers can invite the Holy Spirit to break any burden of the oppressor off of your husband's shoulders. You will be fulfilling the "law of Christ" every time you pray like that, not to mention how it will secure your husband's devotion.

My Prayer to God

LORD, I pray my husband will be able to fully release his burdens to You. I know that when we cast our burdens on You, You will sustain us and not allow us to be shaken (Psalm 55:22 NASB). Help me to bear his burdens in prayer and in any other way You reveal to me. Show me what his greatest burden is and what I can do to lighten it.

I ask that You would relieve him of his heavy load by Your presence in his life. Enable him to understand that when he yokes up with You, You will carry the burden for him. I pray that when he is oppressed by the enemy, whatever prayer or supplication is made by him—when he acknowledges his own burdens before You and turns to You for help—that You will hear him (2 Chronicles 6:29-30). I also pray that as You take his burden from him, he will know it's You doing the heavy lifting.

In Jesus' name I pray.

24

When We Need God's Power on Our Behalf

Your faith should not be
in the wisdom of men
but in the power of God.

1 CORINTHIANS 2:5

HAVE YOU EVER FELT completely powerless in a situation? Have you ever lost control of your car while going downhill on an icy road? Circumstances like that are horrifying because you have absolutely no control. You realize you have power over nothing.

One of the most amazing things about God is that He shares His power with us. He gives us His power to enable us to do things we couldn't normally do. We don't control His power. Only *He* controls it. But we can pray and wait on Him to manifest His power on our behalf. The way to maximize His power in our lives is by living in obedience to His ways. It's the price we must pay for never having to feel powerless.

God doesn't want you and your husband to live "having a form of godliness but denying its power" (2 Timothy 3:5). He wants you to live a life of power. He desires that you see "what is the exceeding greatness of His power" toward all who believe in Him (Ephesians 1:19-21). His power—the power that created the universe, parted the Red Sea, raised Jesus from the dead, restored sight to the blind, and healed diseases and brokenness—is the same power by which God can rescue you out of an impossible situation when you feel powerless to rescue yourself.

If you and your husband find yourselves in an impossible situation and need God to work powerfully on your behalf, lift up praise to Him. Worship Him as the all-powerful God of the universe. Tell Him about the situation in which you feel powerless and ask Him to work a miracle by the power of His Spirit. Thank Him that nothing is impossible with Him. Then trust that when you are sliding down a slippery slope, He will bring you to a place of safety.

My Prayer to God

LORD, I bring before You our most impossible situation. I know we are powerless to do anything to change it, but I also know nothing is impossible for You. I ask that by the power of Your Spirit You would work a miracle in our lives. Give us both great faith to believe You will extend Your power on our behalf. I know You rule the universe by Your power (Psalm 65:6). You saved and redeemed me for all eternity by Your power (Nehemiah 1:10). You raised Jesus from the dead by Your great power: "Though He was crucified in weakness, yet He lives by the power of God" (2 Corinthians 13:4). I know nothing is too hard for You. I praise

You as the all-powerful God of the universe and the Lord of my life.

Your Word says You look over the earth to find people whose hearts are loyal toward You so that You can show Yourself strong on their behalf (2 Chronicles 16:9). My heart is committed to serve You forever, and I praise You and thank You for Your miracle-working power in my life. I know without You I am powerless, but because I have made You Lord over my life, all things are possible—even the transformation of an impossible situation.

In Jesus' name I pray.

25

When I Know I Must Speak Pleasant Words

Pleasant words are like a honeycomb,
sweetness to the soul and health to the bones.

Proverbs 16:24

WHAT ARE THE FIRST WORDS you speak to your spouse when you both get up in the morning? Are they pleasant and positive? Are they covered with the love and joy of the Lord? Or are they powered by yesterday's resentments, disappointments, and unfulfilled expectations? It is of utmost importance that a wife sets the tone of the day for the entire family, but especially for her husband.

It is easy for you as a wife to not be ahead of your emotions and thoughts before you talk to your husband in the morning, especially when you have a lot on your plate, too much to do, you don't feel well, you're upset at your husband, or you haven't had enough time with the Lord to get your heart right. And if you have been up in the night, for whatever reason, and haven't had enough sleep, your mind can be set on a negative track long before your husband wakes up. You may have already thought up many things you want to communicate to him that do not include pleasant words. If you dive in with these issues before he is ready to talk, it can set the day on the wrong course.

The thing to do, right when you wake up in the morning, is ask God to give you pleasant words that bring "sweetness to the soul" of your husband when you first see him—even if you don't think he deserves it at that moment. When God gives you the right attitude first thing in the morning, you'll see what a difference it makes in your day and night. Your husband will respond differently than he would if your words were harsh. A soft word can turn away much suffering and bring great healing. It's not worth it to start your day any other way.

My Prayer to God

LORD, I pray You would help me to pause every morning when I wake up to thank You for the day and ask You to fill me afresh with Your love and joy, so that the first words that come out of my mouth to my husband are pleasant. Help me to hesitate *before* I speak to him for the first time in order to plan how I can set a positive tone for the day. Make me to be a woman with a gentle and loving spirit so that uplifting words flow naturally from me. I pray that the next time I see or talk to my husband, my words will bring sweetness to his soul and health to his body. May they also bring sweetness and health to the very soul of our marriage.

I know there are times when pleasant and sweet is not

my first reaction. I realize I can sometimes worry and allow thoughts and words that are not glorifying to You. At those times I depend on You to transform me so that I can be a strong conduit for Your love to my husband and family. Help me to be a person he wants to be around. Break in me any bad habits of negative, faithless, or critical thinking. Help me to forgive anything he has done or said that is still in my mind. I release the past to You so I can do what is right today. Help me to always consider the state of my heart before I speak.

In Jesus' name I pray.

26

When He Needs Freedom from Destructive Behavior

Be strong in the Lord
and in the power of His might.
Put on the whole armor of God,
that you may be able
to stand against the wiles of the devil.

EPHESIANS 6:10-11

IT'S DIFFICULT FOR A WIFE to see her husband exhibit any kind of destructive behavior. In watching him doing something repeatedly that hurts his health or jeopardizes their family, she sees her future going over a cliff. There can be such terrible consequences for his behavior that it could ruin them financially, as well as destroy him physically or mentally. Whether it is drinking alcohol, taking drugs, gambling, smoking, reckless eating habits, or whatever else she observes her husband doing that could destroy him or endanger her or their children, it can be so heartbreaking to her that she cannot live with it.

Every woman has to decide what she can and cannot tolerate. Life is hard enough without your husband finding ways to make it worse. And she must decide how much she can allow her children to witness before it seriously affects them too.

You may not see behavior as seriously destructive as that in your husband, but perhaps he is taking unnecessary chances with his safety, such as driving too fast, or riding a motorcycle without a helmet, or being careless with dangerous machinery or equipment, or refusing to see a doctor when he should, or not following the doctor's orders and thereby jeopardizing his health. There is only so much you can say or do to try to motivate your husband to stop destructive behavior if he is intent on doing it. But God can do miracles when you fervently pray to Him about it. He hears your prayers, and He wants your husband to be free as much as you do. Your prayers can help your husband open his eyes to see the truth. Your prayers can help him to understand how to put on the whole armor of God so he can stand against these plans of the enemy for his destruction.

My Prayer to God

Lord, I pray You would set my husband free from any destructive behavior he has acquired. Wake him up to the folly of his ways and show him when he is being foolish. Break the chains that bind him and open his blind eyes. Strengthen him where his weakness controls him. Enable him to see when the enemy has erected a stronghold in his life. Help him to understand how his behavior affects me and our children, as well as other family members, coworkers, and friends.

Tell me what I can do to help make this situation better. I know I cannot change him, and I am unable to make anything happen. Only You can open his eyes, deliver him, and set him free from destructive behavior. I know foolish actions are not Your will for his life, and there is a big price to pay for everything that is not Your will. I pray that neither I nor my children will have to pay any price for his careless behavior. Whatever the reason he appears to have little regard for me, our children, or himself by continuing any reckless behavior, I pray You would deliver him from it completely. You are greater and more powerful than whatever draws him away from Your best. I trust You to set him free to be all You made him to be.

In Jesus' name I pray.

27

When We Should Not Rush into Anything

It is not good for a soul to be without knowledge,
and he sins who hastens with his feet.

Proverbs 19:2

FAR TOO OFTEN a hasty decision made without enough knowledge, thought, or prayer has gotten a husband and wife into trouble. And when one spouse is guilty of making that hasty decision over the objections of the other, it can cause serious friction between them. How many times have we, or someone else we know, done something that "seemed like a good idea," but it only *seemed* like a good idea because God was never consulted? The book of Proverbs says, "He who troubles his own house will inherit the wind" (Proverbs 11:29). Doing foolish and impulsive things troubles a spouse, which definitely troubles the house.

If you or your husband has ever rushed into anything without proper consideration, without praying enough about it until you had the leading of the Lord, without talking it out between you, or without gathering all the knowledge and information you needed on the subject, this may have become a prelude to trouble in your house. In fact, it can break down trust in a marriage to the point that it becomes irreparable in the eyes of the spouse who is the sensible one.

No one will continually pay the price for a spouse who does impulsive or irresponsible things that can jeopardize their future. At some point it becomes too much to bear. Pray this doesn't happen to you. Ask God to give you and your husband wisdom in all things. Pray that neither of you ever hastily rushes into something that may be out of God's will for your life.

My Prayer to God

Lord, I pray You would give my husband and me wisdom, knowledge, and understanding so that we don't make hasty decisions without first seeking You for direction. If either of us is ever about to do something like that at any time, I pray You would give us such clear revelation that it stops us in our tracks before we make a serious mistake. Help both of us to never trouble our house by being impulsive and quick to cater to what we *think* is right instead of waiting to hear from You so that we do what we *know* is right.

Don't let us get off the path You have for us by taking even one step in the wrong direction that will lead to problems for us later on. Pull us back from our own way and help us live according to Yours. Keep us from pursuing our own desires over Your will. Wake us up to the truth whenever we have willfully stepped into the path of deception. Keep us from buying something we cannot afford, or committing to something we are not supposed to do, or investing time and money in something You will not bless. Keep our eagerness to have something from controlling our decisions. Give us wisdom, and let our good judgment lead us in the right way. Enable us to have a calm, sensible, Spirit-led approach to every decision we make.

In Jesus' name I pray.

28

When I Must Rethink My Expectations

My soul, wait silently for God alone,
for my expectation is from Him.

PSALM 62:5

WE WIVES TOO OFTEN come into our marriage with great expectations of what our mate is going to be like and who he will become. We see things we *want* to see, and we don't always see the things we *should*. Because our expectations are so high, when our husband doesn't live up to them we can't hide our disappointment. It comes out in moodiness, discontent, disrespect, disdain, critical words, and the ever-popular silent treatment. A wife can become the victim of her own misplaced expectations, and her husband pays for it. King David had it right when he told his soul to wait quietly for the Lord and put his *expectations* in *Him*. We must do the same.

Your husband can only be who he is. You cannot put expectations on him to fulfill you in ways that only God can do. Your husband simply can't be everything to you—nor is he supposed to be—but *God* can be. And He *wants* to be.

Has your husband fulfilled every expectation you have had of him? If not, tell God about it and ask *Him* to fulfill those needs instead. Of course, there are certain expectations you *should* have of your husband, such as fidelity, love, kindness, financial support, protection, and decency. If he cannot, or won't, provide those things for you, he is not living up to what *God* expects of him either. But beyond that, if you are constantly disappointed in your husband, ask God to show you whether you should be looking to your Lord and Savior, instead of your husband, for everything you need.

My Prayer to God

LORD, show me any expectations I have of my husband that are unfair, and for which I should be looking to You to provide instead. I know he cannot meet my every emotional need—and I should not expect him to—but *You* can. I look to You for my comfort, fulfillment, and peace. I thank You for all the good things my husband provides for me, and I ask You to keep me from being critical of him for not being perfect.

Lord, help me to wait quietly for You to provide what I need, for I put all my expectations in You. For everything I have expected from my husband and have been disappointed because he couldn't provide, I now look to You. If I have damaged my husband's self-respect in any way because I have made him feel that I am disappointed in him, I confess that to You as sin. Help me to apologize and make that up to him. Bring restoration, and heal any and all wounds. Where there are certain things I should expect of him as a husband and he has failed to provide, help me to forgive him. I release him into Your hands to become who *You* made him to be and not what I want him to be. Help me to keep my expectations focused on You so I can live free of expectations I have no right to put on him.

In Jesus' name I pray.

29

When He Needs Deliverance from Fear

God has not given us a spirit of fear,
but of power and of love and of a sound mind.

2 TIMOTHY 1:7

JESUS CAME TO DELIVER US from everything that controls our life other than Him. If your husband's life is in any way controlled by something other than the Holy Spirit, he must have deliverance from that. If he has a tormenting fear, he needs the perfect love of God to set him free of it. The Bible says, "There is no fear in love; but perfect love casts out fear, because fear involves torment. But he who fears has not been made perfect in love" (1 John 4:18). Pray for the love of God to perfectly fill your husband's heart, soul, and mind and evaporate all fear from his life.

There are many things in this world to be afraid of, and it is wise to have enough sensible fear to keep yourself and your family safe. For example, you should have enough fear of predators to keep your children away from strangers. In that way fear can be protective because it keeps you and your family out of harm's way. But a spirit of fear is oppressive because it controls our lives.

Ask God to show you where your husband is in any way controlled by fear. He cannot make sound decisions if he is motivated by fear, for that is opposite of moving with the leading of the Lord. If you ever see that happening in your husband, pray for him to be free of all ungodly fear. Say to him, or pray over him, the words, "God has not given you a spirit of fear; He has given you love, power, and a sound mind. Refuse anything but the sound mind God has given you." God does not want you or your husband to live in fear. That is not His will for your life. He wants you both to live in fear of *Him*—fear meaning *reverence* here. He wants you to live in His love, and by His power, and with the sound mind He has given you.

My Prayer to God

LORD, I pray You would deliver my husband from all fear. Whenever he is controlled by fear, liberate him to know You in such depth that Your love perfects him and casts out all fear. Keep him from making decisions motivated by fear rather than being led by Your Spirit. Take away any fear that oppresses, alters, or limits his life. Help him to understand that freedom is found in Your presence. I pray that when he is set free, he will recognize it is You who liberated him and he will give You the glory. I know that when You set him free, he is free forever.

I pray You would set *me* free from all fear as well. Wherever Your love has not been perfected in me so that I am free from all fear, I pray You would overflow me with Your liberating love that brings wholeness. Help me to overcome all my fear so I can be a support and encouragement to my husband in overcoming his. I know fear indicates a lack of faith in Your ability to take care of us. Strengthen our faith to believe that we have not received the spirit of bondage (Romans 8:15). Instead, we have received a Savior who loves us to wholeness.

In Jesus' name I pray.

30

When We Must Recognize the Enemy's Lies

Submit to God.
Resist the devil and he will flee from you.

James 4:7

We all have a spiritual enemy. For those who don't know or believe that, their ability to identify the enemy's work in their lives and resist it will be nonexistent. The enemy wants to destroy marriages because God has joined together the people in them in order to glorify Him.

The enemy comes "to steal, and to kill, and to destroy" (John 10:10). He is the author of lies. "He is a liar and the father of it" (John 8:44). By enticing you to believe his lies, he can steal your joy, kill your love, and destroy your relationship. He will speak thoughts into your mind that contradict the Word of God, that play on your insecurities and doubts, and cause miscommunication between you and your husband. He will feed you suspicious and critical thoughts and try to make you think that his lies are true and that God's truth is a lie.

When something happens between you and your husband to undermine or threaten your marriage, ask God to help you discern how much is due to works of the flesh and how much is the plan of the enemy in operation. Then take steps to resist both. Pray often that you and your husband will have the ability to recognize the enemy's lies. In order to do that, you must have a clear knowledge of God's truth. So fill your mind and soul with His Word. Ask Him to show you clearly what is true and what is not. Keep praying and God will reveal this to you. Resist the enemy by choosing to live in obedience to God's ways and by worshipping God for who He is. The enemy hates that and has to flee from you.

My Prayer to God

LORD, I pray You would help my husband and me to discern the lies of the enemy—especially when there is strife or tension between us. Open our eyes to recognize any spirit of division or confusion as the enemy's plan to divert us away from the plans of God. On behalf of my husband, I submit our lives to You. Help us to surrender to You in every way and choose to live according to Your laws. Teach us to submit to You by reading and speaking Your Word so that it is implanted in our hearts and becomes part of our lives as we live in obedience to it. Help us to submit to You in prayer, in praise, in worship, and in gratitude.

I pray whenever my husband and I have a disagreement that turns to strife, or have unholy attitudes, suspicions, and criticisms that destroy our unity, that we will stop and say, "Enough! We refuse to allow any spirit other than the Holy Spirit to have a place of influence in our lives." Thank You, Lord, that You have given us victory over all the plans of the enemy. Thank You that he has to flee from our lives when we expose his plans to the light. Give us both wisdom to identify the enemy's work in our lives and the power to resist him.

In Jesus' name I pray.

31

When I Long to Excel in What I Do

She watches over the ways of her household,
and does not eat the bread of idleness.
Her children rise up and call her blessed;
her husband also, and he praises her:
"Many daughters have done well,
but you excel them all."

PROVERBS 31:27-29

EVERY WOMAN—married or not—wants to excel in all she does. Whether her work is to take care of children and manage her house, or she is a highly paid CEO of a corporation—or somewhere in between—she wants to do it effectively. Don't ever underestimate the importance of the work you do to build your home. Even if you are working full time at a job outside your house, or you are not working outside your home at all, everything you do *in* your home is important and you want to do it well.

If you find fulfillment, purpose, joy, and reward in each day's work, you gain strength instead of being depleted. You are excited about life instead of lethargic. You are more interesting and enjoyable to be around. The way to excel in all you do is to submit your work to the Lord. He can take even the most difficult, challenging, or boring aspects of it and turn it into something meaningful and productive.

Every woman wants to be a great wife, mother, creator of a home, and worker at a job, occupation, or career, or whatever God has given her to do. This doesn't mean being all things to all people. It means being your best for your family and depending on God to help you excel in everything you do each day.

My Prayer to God

Lord, I pray You would bless everything I do. Help me to understand all You have for me to accomplish and enable me to do it well. Show me how to find purpose in even the most difficult or mundane aspects of my work. Reveal exactly what my work is to be, and enable me to accomplish it beyond what I know I can do on my own. If I need to make any changes in all I do, show me what I should be doing instead. Give me the energy and clarity of mind to make those changes.

With regard to my work outside our home, help me to find favor with those I come in contact with in the process. Teach me better and more efficient ways to do what I need to accomplish. Help me to have a great attitude about whatever it is I am doing at the time—whether it is maintaining a home, working at a job, or running a business—so that I can always do my best. Above all, I need to have a clear sense of Your purpose in my life and of the gifts You have put in me. I want to know I am always in the right place doing the very thing You would have me do. Enable me to sense Your presence guiding me every step of the way. If my work right now is to establish our home and raise children, help me to find all the great fulfillment and satisfaction You have for me in that. Enable me to excel in everything I do so that I can be a blessing to my family and others. Most of all, I want to know that what I am doing pleases You.

In Jesus' name I pray.

32

When He Needs a Change of Mind

Do not be conformed to this world,
but be transformed by the renewing of your mind,
that you may prove what is that good and
acceptable and perfect will of God.

ROMANS 12:2

WE ALL NEED TO periodically have our minds renewed, recharged, and changed. Each one of us can get into habits of thought that are off, and we may even be blind to the fact that it's happening. Our thought habits profoundly affect who we are and what we become. If we are more affected by a godless world than we are by the kingdom of God, it will have a profound effect on our marriage relationship, where it is crucial that we have the Spirit of God influencing our mind at all times.

The world encroaches upon us every day in some way if we are not vigilant. Pray for your husband to recognize that and be drawn toward the goodness, greatness, and power of God in his life. While a wife cannot always change her husband's mind, she *can* pray to her husband's heavenly Father to bring about a desire in him to not conform to the world's system of thinking, but rather to the Lord's ways.

You must pray frequently for your husband's mind because you don't know what thoughts can creep into his thinking, sometimes without him even realizing it. If you ever see that his thinking is off or not lining up with God's truth, pray that God will give him the mind of Christ and change his mind forever. Ask God to renew your husband's mind so he will not conform to this world, but will instead "prove what is that good and acceptable and perfect will of God."

My Prayer to God

LORD, I pray You would bring about a change in my husband's mind. Take away any desire for the things of the world and replace it with a desire for more of You and Your kingdom. Renew his thoughts so that they are pleasing in Your sight. If what he is thinking is not acceptable to You, expose that to the light of Your truth. Enable him to see the error of his plans and considerations. Wherever he has gotten off the path You have for him in his thought life, reveal that to him in ways he can clearly see. Don't let him accept worldly attitudes and mind-sets that will lead him astray. Only You, Lord, know his thoughts. And only You can transform them and line them up according to Your will for his life.

I know how a wrong thought, when it is accepted as truth, can lead us away from all You have for us. Don't let that happen to him. Don't let that happen to me, either. Open our eyes to see the truth so we can reject any deception we may be under. Where there is a specific issue that I truly feel my husband needs to have a change of mind about, I ask You to either renew his mind completely about that or show me if am wrong and therefore should seek Your renewal in *my* mind instead. Thank You for giving us the mind of Christ. Help us to rely on You and the truth of Your Word imprinted on our heart.

In Jesus' name I pray.

33

When We Must Make Each Other a Priority

Many waters cannot quench love,
nor can the floods drown it.
If a man would give for love
all the wealth of his house,
it would be utterly despised.

SONG OF SOLOMON 8:7

AS SOLOMON SAID, none of the situations that wash over our lives can put out the flame of love, nor can problems drown it. If you had to give up everything for the love of your life, the wealth you had would be worth nothing to you. And if you kept your wealth and gave up your love, you would come to despise your wealth. Nothing that you have—or have to do—is worth more than the love between you and your husband. That's why you must make each other a priority.

We all know how easy it is to devote so much time to work,

career, business, children, friends, church, or various activities that we neglect each other. In our busy lives, it takes a concentrated and specific effort to stay connected to each other in deep and meaningful ways. But when you both are drowning in exhaustion at the end of the day and flooded with stress and preoccupation, meaningful connecting with your spouse may seem like more effort than you have the strength to put into it. But your love may be drowning and your heart flooded with regret if you don't. And if love fades or dies, it's devastating. If that has happened to you, ask God to help you both become each other's priority again. Even if it *hasn't* happened, ask God to help you *continue* to make each other a top priority.

If you haven't been each other's top priority for a while, ask God to enable you to break that cycle and start devoting time to each other. Even if you feel the marriage has died and it is too late, God can resurrect it. It is one of His specialties. Invite the Holy Spirit to rekindle your love and communication. No matter how busy and tired you are, set aside time together alone. Dinner out once a week is so much cheaper than a marriage counselor or a divorce lawyer. The money you save by not doing that will mean nothing if you lose the love of your life.

My Prayer to God

Lord, I pray You would help my husband and me to make each other a priority. Teach us to lay down our work and responsibilities for special times to be together alone. I know we cannot have the marriage You want us to have if we are never spending quality time together. Enable us to affirm each other by communicating the deep thoughts and feelings that need to be expressed and seldom are because there just isn't time or inclination. Remind each of us why we chose to marry in the first place.

Keep our love and attraction for each other alive so that we don't allow each other to slip from a place of top priority. Where that has already happened, help us to change it by deliberately setting aside time for each other, to build each other up, and to clear the air of any miscommunication or unloving thoughts we have acquired. Help us to take the time to peacefully talk everything out so we are current on all emotions and no specter of the past can rise up to steal our joy. Most of all, enable us to fully treasure each other more than all the wealth that we have, or people that we know, or dreams that we follow.

In Jesus' name I pray.

34

When I Want Reassurance of My Place in the Marriage

A man shall leave his father and mother
and be joined to his wife,
and they shall become one flesh.

GENESIS 2:24

TOO OFTEN WHEN WOMEN READ the Bible, certain passages that have the word "man" in them *seem* to say that it is not applicable to a woman. While there are a number of Scriptures where this is true—such as the one above—the Bible also says, "He created them male and female, and blessed them and *called them Mankind* in the day they were created" (Genesis 5:2, emphasis added). From the beginning we were made in God's image and were called "Mankind"—later in common usage it was shortened to *man*. When we refer to "all mankind," we are not just talking about men and excluding women. The Bible says of the great flood, "All flesh died that moved on the earth...

and every man" (Genesis 7:21). This doesn't mean only men died and women didn't. "Man" means every person.

It's important for women understand this, because if we don't we can acquire an attitude that says, "It's a man's world and I will always be thought of as second class in comparison." And, granted, in the *world* in many instances and situations this is true. But in the eyes of God, you and your husband are one. God sees you as equal. He gives you different responsibilities in the relationship, but one is not less important than the other.

God calls you to submit to your husband not because you are less than he is, but because ultimately one person has to lead and one has to submit themselves to the leader. The husband leads, but he has to submit himself to God, and he is accountable to God. You are accountable to God too, but your husband is accountable to God for the decisions he makes that concern *you*. I know submission is very hard for a wife to accept when her husband has made some decisions that impact her in a negative way. But arguing over this, beyond making your opinion and feelings known, will only further impact the situation negatively. Better to ask God to redeem what has happened and help you to trust Him in the process.

My Prayer to God

LORD, help me to understand what my rightful place of authority is in our marriage. I see from Your Word that You made a husband and wife to be one, yet You have set boundaries where the husband must lead and the wife must submit. Sometimes I find it hard to submit to a bad or wrong decision—especially when it drastically affects me and our family. I pray that when I have these kinds of concerns, You would help me to make them known to my husband without being overbearing or out of order.

Teach us both to have a conversation without an argument. Help me to choose my words carefully when my thoughts need to be expressed. Give my husband ears to hear You advising him and a heart that listens when I share my thoughts. Show me how to be rightly submissive while still taking the authority You have given me in prayer. If my husband makes a bad decision against my expressed wishes, help me to forgive him and, above all, trust *You* to protect me. I know that he answers to You concerning the way he leads our family. Help us to work together as one and not as opposing factions.

In Jesus' name I pray.

35

When He Needs the Leading of God About His Occupation

Do you see a man who excels in his work?
He will stand before kings;
he will not stand before unknown men.

PROVERBS 22:29

HOW MANY TIMES have we seen a man whose wife is working to support him while he pursues a dream of his own making that God is not blessing? And the result is an unbearable strain on her and the marriage. Or how many men are frustrated in their work and are irritable because of it? Every man needs to know he is doing the right work. Even if it is only a temporary job that will lead to the ultimate work God has called him to do, he needs the confidence of knowing he is following the leading of the Holy Spirit and moving in the will of God. This is why you must pray about the work your husband does.

First of all, pray that your husband understands the gifts God has put in him. Pray that he hears from God about what he is supposed to be doing with those gifts. Pray also that he will understand what his calling is, so that his gifts never take priority over his calling. Part of who he is called to be is your husband, and his gifts should never take priority over that.

Whatever your husband's situation is now—whether he is out of work, has the greatest job, or is somewhere in between—pray that he is moving in the will of God. If he is not in the right place, or he has a job that is not pleasing to the Lord, ask God to reveal that to you both. If he is doing work that is not God's will, ask the Lord to take him out of it and move him into what he was created to do. If he is in a job he dislikes and it is depleting him, ask God to help him either find peace and purpose in it or move him into something better. Pray that once your husband knows the leading of the Lord, he will follow it.

My Prayer to God

LORD, I pray You would enable my husband to hear Your voice speaking to him regarding his work. Lead him to do what You want him to do. Reveal to him the gifts You have put in him so that he is not pursuing something You will not bless. If he is where he's supposed to be, enable him to find favor with the people for whom he works. If a change needs to be made, I pray You would show him what to do and when to do it. Teach him to seek to know Your perfect will.

In every meeting he has, I pray You would be in charge so he will hear Your voice over all others. Enable him to make the right decisions with regard to his work. Only You, Lord, know what is ahead at this time in our lives and in our world. Teach him to pursue the right things at the right time. Enable him to hear Your voice saying, "This is the way, walk in it" (Isaiah 30:21). I pray he will find great fulfillment, satisfaction, and success in his work, along with the confidence of knowing he is doing what You have called him to do. May his gifts always make room for him and bring him before great men (Proverbs 18:16).

In Jesus' name I pray.

36

When We Must Get Out of Debt

Owe no one anything except
to love one another,
for he who loves another
has fulfilled the law.

Romans 13:8

Living under a mountain of debt will suffocate any marriage—especially if one person did not want the debt and didn't accumulate it but is the one working to pay it off. This is a setup for disaster. Debt is overwhelming, and it has been the ruin of countless marriages. Every effort must be made to eliminate debt before it crushes you, because it is a burden your shoulders were not meant to carry.

Becoming debt free must be a priority in both of your lives until you actually are free. From that point, *staying* debt free is your constant goal. Having a mortgage and a car loan are fine when you know you can easily make the payments for both. And putting a vacation or certain purchases on a credit card for convenience works when you know you can pay them off right away. But carrying debt month after month, one finance charge after another, is no way to live.

Ask God to give you and your husband the wisdom to manage your finances well. If you need professional help, there are a number of good Christian financial advisors and excellent books to read on the subject. Most of all, pray that you and your husband will be in agreement about how your finances are handled. Agree to pay off all bills every month. Agree to save a certain amount. Agree to not make major purchases until you know you have the finances to pay for them. Careless spending is one of the biggest deal breakers in a marriage. Ask God to help you avoid that or enable you to get out of debt if it has already happened. One of the consequences for backbreaking debt is that it will break the back of your marriage too.

My Prayer to God

Lord, I pray You will help my husband and me to pay off all our debts. Give us wisdom about our finances so that we don't spend more than we make and never incur more debt than we have the money to cover. Give us the discipline to save for the future—especially future situations that are unforeseen. Teach us how to handle our money, always remembering that everything we have comes from You (1 Corinthians 4:7). Where we could benefit from a Christian financial counselor, show us whom to go to or whose book to read on the subject. Most of all, I pray You would help us to face all financial matters openly and together, always remembering that we are on the same team.

Enable us to pay off all credit cards and only use them wisely so our money is not wasted on finance charges. Help us to live within our means and not strive for a lifestyle above what we can afford or sustain. Enable us to be strong and not spend money on what we don't need, but rather spend money only as we are directed by Your Holy Spirit. Teach us to give to You the way You want us to so that we never limit the blessings You have for us. I submit our finances to You and ask that You be in charge of them and all our decisions and expenses. Give us the desire to follow You and not the desires of our flesh.

In Jesus' name I pray.

37

When I Need to Show More Affection

Let the husband render to his wife
the affection due her,
and likewise also the wife to her husband.

1 CORINTHIANS 7:3

FOR MANY PEOPLE who were not raised with open affection, showing it can be difficult. It's not that they don't feel affectionate. In fact, often they have very deep feelings of love and affection for their spouse, but they find it difficult to show it in ways that may be meaningful. But showing affection is not just about doing what we *feel comfortable* doing; it is a matter of *obeying God.*

If your husband is not as affectionate as you would like him to be, ask God to do a miracle of healing in his heart. If he was not shown affection as a child, God can heal that. It's easier for him to be affectionate to his wife when he is free of hurts from the past and he feels good in his skin. This is not a false confidence that pumps him up in a superficial way. It is genuinely feeling good about who God made him to be, and sensing the love and affection of God so much that it overflows to his wife automatically.

If you are the one who tends to be less affectionate than your husband would like, ask God to help you with that. Pray that you will be healed of all wounds of the past where you were not shown the proper affection by the people who were supposed to care for you. Ask God to show you what you can do for your husband that would make him feel loved. It's hard to do something you haven't learned naturally. But this is what God requires of you, so it has to be something you have the capability of giving and He can enable you to do. If you are willing, God will help you do it.

My Prayer to God

Lord, I pray You would help me show the affection that my husband needs and that You want me to extend to him. I don't want to be selfish in that regard, nor do I want to be ignoring any of Your requirements. Teach me ways to show affection that would be a blessing to him. The ways I would like my husband to show affection to me are in the affirming words he speaks to me, in the considerate things he does, and in a gentle touch. Help me to show affection to him in those ways too. I pray that affection would flow out of me so that it doesn't feel forced or contrived. Take away any self-consciousness I have about that and make it a natural outpouring of kindness, the source of which is Your Spirit in me.

Show us both ways to be affectionate that we might not otherwise think of. Where there has been hurt, neglect, or damage in our past that makes it difficult for either of us to show "the affection due" each other, I pray You would heal us and bring us to a place of wholeness. Fill us with Your love so that it flows out of each of us toward the other. Take away any hurts we have inflicted on each other and heal those wounds so that we feel comfortable being affectionate. Take away any selfish withholding of affection that I have. I don't want to do anything that keeps me from obeying You. Pour Your love out in me so it overflows from me to him and causes open affection to be a natural consequence.

In Jesus' name I pray.

38

When He Must Be Gone a Short Time

The Lord shall preserve you from all evil;
He shall preserve your soul.
The Lord shall preserve your going out
and your coming in
from this time forth, and even forevermore.

PSALM 121:7-8

WHEN YOUR HUSBAND GOES out of town on a business trip, or a weekend of fun and recreation with the guys, if things have been going badly between you, it can be a relief that he is gone and you have the house to yourself. It gives you a chance to think things through and remember why you got married in the first place. If everything has been going well with you both, a short time of separation can still be a good thing if you need a chance to miss each other. Whatever your situation, this is a valuable time to pray for him.

When he is gone, first of all pray for his protection in planes, trains, automobiles, and boats. Second, pray for him to be protected from the evil one (2 Thessalonians 3:3). A man can fall prey to many enticements when he is away from home and in another world. Pray that your husband will keep himself from anything the enemy would like to put in front of him and not violate any of God's laws (1 John 5:18).

Even if your husband is not out of town now or won't be going away soon, pray all this in advance of the next time he goes away for a short time. Pray that your husband will be in God's hands every step of the way and that he will return home safely (Psalm 18:2). Ask God to bring him back refreshed, renewed, and happy to be home and seeing you. Pray that not only will God go with *him*, but that *he* will go with God.

My Prayer to God

LORD, I pray You will protect my husband whenever he is away. Keep him safe in cars and planes and every other mode of transportation. Bring him back home safely. Bless all that he does—whether for business or fun. I pray in that time away he will draw closer to You. Help him to hear Your voice speaking to his heart. Even though we are apart, I pray You will enable us to grow closer. Help us to let go of any problems or disagreements we have had in the past, and dwell on the good things we have together now and in our future.

Enable my husband to be influenced by You and Your ways more than anyone or any influence with which he may come in contact. Help him to turn to You as his rock, fortress, and deliverer. Keep him on the path of obedience to

You so that he will be protected from the evil one. Guard his health and his soul. Preserve his going out and his coming home. I pray when he returns that we find greater compatibility and communication than we had before. I also pray that the separation will have been a time of rejuvenation for both of us, and that we will each have a fresh perspective and greater insight. Enable us to see each other with new eyes. I release him into Your hands today for safekeeping.

In Jesus' name I pray.

39

When We Want Freedom from Depression

O Lord, You brought my soul
up from the grave; You have kept me alive,
that I should not go down to the pit.

Psalm 30:3

Whether it is you or your husband who is depressed, it is something that should never be ignored. Those feelings don't often go away on their own, and in fact can be pushed down only to rise again more powerfully than ever. There are many reasons either you or your husband can feel depressed, but whatever the cause, depression should be prayed about until it is gone. It's good to pray *with* each other about it, unless you feel he would not want to do that.

Usually depression happens to one person and not the other, but it *can* happen to both at once. In that case, find someone who has the maturity and decency to keep a confidence, and then ask that person to pray with you both about it. Don't do nothing. Ask God to reveal the root of the depression to you and show you how to pray. Ask Him if either of you need professional help. You may have a physical or chemical imbalance that needs to be corrected. With all the stress in our lives, it's a wonder we all don't have some kind of imbalance. There are doctors who can help with that.

The bottom line is God has the power to set you free. He can do it through a sovereign act of His delivering and healing power, and He can do it through a Christian counselor, a psychologist, or a psychiatrist. No matter how or when He does it, prayer must lay the foundation for it to happen. Ask for the freedom from depression God has for you and don't stop praying until you have it.

My Prayer to God

Lord, I pray that if either my husband or I ever feel depressed, You would clearly show us how to pray and what to do about it. Help us to never just accept depression as a way of life, but rather enable us to see it as far from the way You want us to live. Whenever either one of us is suffering with chronic depression or sadness that seems to overtake us and not let up, show us if we need professional help from a Christian counselor, psychologist, or psychiatrist. Reveal if there is any imbalance in our system that is causing it and what to do about it. If there is something we need to do or stop doing, I pray You would show us clearly. Whatever the course of action, I pray You would set us totally and completely free.

Where depression has come upon either of us because of

depressing circumstances, I pray You would break its power in our lives. Enable us to rise above our situation and the sadness it has brought and refuse to let it control or grip us. Give each of us the ability to possess our own souls and refuse anything that attempts to influence us other than Your Spirit (Luke 21:19). Enable us to walk wisely so that we will be delivered (Proverbs 28:26). Bring us up from the pit and set us on the rock. Put Your song in our hearts (Psalm 40:1-3). Heal my husband's soul and mine, and lead us on the path of wholeness You have for us (Psalm 23:3).

In Jesus' name I pray.

40

When I Find It Difficult to Trust Him

Trust in the Lord with all your heart,
and lean not on your own understanding.

PROVERBS 3:5

HAS YOUR HUSBAND ever done something you feel has violated your trust in him? It doesn't have to be anything as terrible as infidelity. It could be financial irresponsibility, or some kind of lie or deception, or hurtful treatment of you, or a confidence he shared with someone else. Whatever it is, you can find yourself wary—always suspecting he may do the same thing again. Yet there must be trust in your marriage relationship or you can never move forward.

Living in such a close relationship without trust is not living at all. It's remarkably sad to not be able to trust the one we are supposed to trust the most. If this has happened to you, it must be remedied, rectified, and resolved. Only God can truly restore the kind of trust you need to have.

If your husband has done something to lose your trust, pray that God will lead him to complete repentance. Pray also that your heart will be willing to forgive him. This can be especially hard if he is a repeat offender, but it is not too hard for God to work forgiveness in your heart if you are willing. Ask God to set you free of all anger, frustration, disappointment, fear, and resentment. The most important thing to do after you have prayed for your husband's repentance and your forgiveness is to pray you will trust God to work a miracle in your husband's heart and yours as well. You have to first decide that You will trust God with all your heart and not lean on your own understanding. Then He will enable you to trust your husband again.

My Prayer to God

LORD, I confess any time when I have lost faith in my husband and don't have full trust in him. I know that is not the way You want me to live. Help us both to have faith in each other and not live in constant distrust, bracing ourselves for what violation of trust is going to happen next. Where my distrust is unfounded, I pray You would help me to see that and enable me to step out in trust of him again. Where my distrust is legitimate because he has truly violated that trust, I ask for a miracle of restoration.

First of all, I pray You would lead my husband to total repentance. Bring him to his knees before You in confession so he can be restored. I pray he will be sincerely apologetic to me as well. Second, help me to forgive him so completely that I can trust him fully without reservation again. And last, but most important of all, help me to trust You with all my heart to rectify this situation. Work powerfully in my husband to make him trustworthy, and do a work in me to make me trusting. Help me to not depend on my own reasoning, but rather to depend on Your ability to transform us both.

In Jesus' name I pray.

41

When He Must Sow in the Spirit and Not the Flesh

Walk in the Spirit, and you shall not fulfill the lust of the flesh.

GALATIANS 5:16

WHATEVER SEEDS WE SOW will determine what we reap in life. Anyone who "sows to his flesh will of the flesh reap corruption," but when we sow to the Spirit, we "reap everlasting life" (Galatians 6:8).

Too often what we are living out in our lives is in direct correlation to what we have sown. However, when you are married, *you* will *also* live in the harvest of what your husband has sown. And he will live in what you have sown as well. If he has sown seeds of irresponsibility and carelessness with finances, you will live in what that brings about in your life. If you have sown seeds of deception, then you *both* will experience the harvest that results from that. This is not to say if your husband has done something terrible or illegal that God won't protect you in it. He will. But you do have to pray for that. Things don't just automatically happen that way.

Sowing and reaping are a given—a sure thing. If your husband sows to the wind, you will both reap the whirlwind unless you pray for God to protect you from that. And even then, you can still be affected by it if there is not repentance on the part of the one who has sown poorly. Ask God to help you and your husband sow seeds of whatever you both want to reap in your life. Pray that God will help you do what is necessary to reap a life of peace, happiness, purpose, abundance, and love. Ask God to enable you both to walk in the Holy Spirit so you will not fulfill the lust of your flesh.

My Prayer to God

Lord, I pray You will help my husband to always sow good seeds that will positively affect our lives together. Help him to sow good seeds in his work and his finances so we can reap financial security and stability. Help him to plant good seeds in his relationships and in his words and actions so that he reaps the respect and appreciation of others. You have said that if we will "not grow weary while doing good" that "in due season we shall reap if we do not lose heart" (Galatians 6:9). Strengthen him to never grow weary of doing what is right. Give him the understanding that he does not have to take things into his own hands, but it is better to always do things *Your* way so that his reward will be a harvest of good. Help him to learn well that doing things *his* way, without Your leading, never works.

Teach him to sow for good and not for evil, for right and not for wrong, for You and not for selfishness. Enable him to clearly understand the difference. Put a holy barometer in him that registers clearly in his spirit when he is tipping toward sowing in the flesh and not the spirit. Strengthen him so that he is strong enough to refuse discouragement, knowing that if he has sown well, Your harvest of blessing is guaranteed for the future. Help him to not grow tired of waiting for the harvest.

In Jesus' name I pray.

42

When We Seek Protection from Sexual Immorality

Flee sexual immorality.
Every sin that a man does is outside the body,
but he who commits sexual immorality
sins against his own body.

1 CORINTHIANS 6:18

SEXUAL SIN IS WORSE than other sins because it has consequences in our own body. Being that our body is the temple of the Holy Spirit, that means sexual sin of any kind—even in the mind—causes great conflict within us, for how can dark live alongside light? One of the ways to avoid sexual temptation is to stay close to God and His Word. The other is not to neglect the sexual needs of your spouse. Sexual intimacy is an important way to bring unity into your marriage. Joining your hearts, minds, and bodies breaks down any stronghold of separation between you and reaffirms your oneness.

Your husband most likely is out working in the world where a spirit of lust is everywhere. He needs your prayers for protection and the strength to resist it when it presents itself. The same is true for you too. It is dangerous to think that sexual failure cannot happen to you or your husband in a moment of weakness or vulnerability—even if it is only in the mind. Thoughts have consequences, and that's why God tells us to take every thought captive. We have to take charge of our mind in order to stay undeceived. There is no safe place where infidelity, or the idea of it, cannot reveal itself as an option.

If infidelity has already happened to one of you, ask God for His healing and restoring power to work a miracle of deliverance, forgiveness, and restoration in both of you. And get help. This is too big an issue to go through alone.

Ask God to enable you and your husband to see to it that this important area of your life is not polluted by neglect, selfishness, busyness, or the inability to keep your eyes from evil. Seek God for the strength to flee sexual sin—even if you think this can never happen to you. That story is way too familiar.

My Prayer to God

LORD, I pray You will help my husband and me to resist sexual temptation of any kind, even in the mind. Strengthen us so we will not surrender to the lust of the world that strives to keep us dissatisfied with what we have. Protect us from being lured to look and wonder, or to succumb and wander. Help us to flee at the first sign of any possibility of sexual sin and run immediately to You. Give us eyes to see what is truly happening even *before* it happens so that we can avoid the deception of immorality. Teach us how to maintain control over our own body, mind, and soul so that we are ever mindful of the purity You want us to live in (1 Thessalonians 4:3-5).

Where either of us has fallen into sexual immorality in the past—even if only in the mind—I pray You would set us completely free from the severe bondage of that. Work a miracle of restoring trust and forgiveness between us. Only You have the power to free us from the debilitating sense of betrayal and can restore us to a new beginning. Keep us both strong in faith, in self-control, in Your Word, and in Your presence so that sexual sin is never a part of our future.

In Jesus' name I pray.

43

When I Need to Show Him Honor and Respect

Let each one of you in particular
so love his own wife as himself,
and let the wife see that she respects her husband.

EPHESIANS 5:33

GOD MAKES IT CLEAR that a wife is supposed to respect her husband. Having respect is crucial to a man. It's important for a wife to *receive* respect from her husband too, but perhaps it is mentioned here specifically as a wife's responsibility because we women can forget to show it. This same verse instructs the husband to *love* his wife. Could it also be that a husband may easily neglect to show the love his wife needs? It's not that he doesn't love her; it's just that he forgets to show it. Love and respect for each other in a marriage are definitely the will of God, and the will of God is something we always need to pray about.

It is very damaging for a man to not be respected, just as it is damaging for a woman to not feel loved. You may greatly respect your husband, but if you do not deliberately show it, he may feel that you don't. Respect can be diminished in one major incident, or it can be eroded over time. Be diligent to see that neither of these happens to you. If it already has, ask God to help you regain proper respect for your husband, and in the meantime be able to treat him with the respect God wants you to have. The respect issue is such an enormous one that you cannot let it slide. A husband needs respect from his wife, and if she can't or won't show it, he may try to find it elsewhere.

Pray that there is a free exchange of love and respect in your marriage, because neither of you will do well without that affirmation. Ask God to show you ways your husband needs to be built up with assurance of your respect for him, both for who he is and what he does. Your respect makes him feel valued, and that is a great investment in the longevity and health of your marriage.

My Prayer to God

Lord, I pray You will help me to show respect toward my husband in the way You want me to. Where my respect for him has been lowered, I pray You would restore it. Where there have been things he has done, or not done, that have eroded my respect, I confess my judgmental attitude and lack of mercy. Where I have perceived in him a clear lack of respect for me, and this has diminished him in my eyes, I confess that to You as sin. For I know that reciprocity is not Your way, and getting even is never acceptable in Your eyes.

Help me to see my husband the way You do—as one

of Your children. Reveal to me any time I have not esteemed him the way I should and this has contributed to a growing wall between us. Where I have closed off my heart to him in order to avoid being hurt, I confess that to You as well. Forgive me and teach me ways to show respect for him in a manner that will clearly communicate it. Enable me to dwell on the good in him and what he has done, and pray to You about the things that have troubled me.

In Jesus' name I pray.

44

When He Has Lost Vision for Tomorrow

Where there is no vision, the people perish:
but he that keepeth the law, happy is he.

PROVERBS 29:18 KJV

WHEN YOUR HUSBAND loses his vision for a bright tomorrow, it means he has lost sight of his purpose and his reason to get up in the morning. He has misplaced his sense of God's calling on his life and his reason to keep fighting the good fight. (Or perhaps he never had a sense of his purpose and calling in the first place.) He may also have lost his reason to keep working and trying. He can even lose his drive to face the day. Having a husband who has lost sight of his future—or your future together—is not a good thing. The Bible says people can't survive without a vision. That's why the enemy of our soul comes to steal away the vision we have from God, so that he can kill our hope and destroy our sense of purpose. But your prayers for your husband to have a clear vision for his future and your future together can restore all that and make an enormous difference in his life.

Lack of vision happens gradually. It creeps in a day at a time, a thought at a time, a disappointment at a time. And it can happen to anyone. We get too busy. We get discouraged or exhausted. We work too hard for too long. We try to do right, but things keep going wrong. This could be happening to your husband right now without either of you even realizing it. If you're not certain how your husband feels about the future, ask him and then pray accordingly. If you can tell he has lost his vision, your prayer can help him find it and be able to hear from God again.

My Prayer to God

LORD, I pray You would give my husband a clear and strong vision for the future—not only *his* future, but also our future together as a couple. If the many challenges he has faced, or the disappointments he has experienced, have accumulated enough to take away his sense of hopeful anticipation, I pray You would help him to see that his future is in You and not in outside circumstances. Give him the understanding he needs to know that the value of his life and purpose are not determined by external situations. Enable him to see that success is not in how well things are going at the moment, but it's in how close he walks with You in prayer and in Your Word. Help him to understand that true vision for his life and our lives together comes only from You.

When my husband is feeling hopeless, I pray he would realize that his hope is found in You. Where his vision has become clouded because of futile thoughts, wrong actions, or advanced apathy, I pray You would enable him to comprehend that he is wholly dependent upon You for proper thinking and right actions. Where he has overworked or overworried, I pray You would revive him again. Even if he doesn't know specifics about his future, help him recognize that he has a bright one. Don't allow him to waste away in his own disappointments. Restore his spiritual sight so he can see that his future is found in You.

In Jesus' name I pray.

45

When We Need to Remember the Purpose of Family

Did He not make them one,
having a remnant of the Spirit?
And why one? He seeks godly offspring.
Therefore take heed to your spirit,
and let none deal treacherously
with the wife of his youth.

MALACHI 2:15

THE PURPOSE OF A FAMILY—a husband, wife, and children—is to glorify God. For those of you who do not have children, for whatever reason, I am not mentioning this to make you feel bad or self-conscious about that. Paul did not have children or a wife because God had another plan for him. Perhaps He has another plan for you. He used Paul in a powerful way that would not have been possible if he was a husband and a father. He is surely using you in that same way. If you have peace about not having children, then God has something else for you to do. If you don't have peace, then ask God to either give you a child or else give you the peace you need about not having a child. He will do that.

With that said, the simple truth about the purpose of marriage is to have "godly offspring" who will grow up to glorify Him. The message in this section of Scripture is that the husband is not to "deal treacherously" with his wife and treat her badly, because the Lord sees all that goes on in your marriage (Malachi 2:13-14). He knows how your husband treats you, as well as how you treat him. But God lays the responsibility right in the husband's lap. He expects the husband to honor the covenant of marriage by treating his wife well.

You both made a covenant before God when you married, and now you are *one* in His sight. And it is your husband's responsibility to love you as he loves himself because you are part of him and he is part of you. When he does that, you can glorify God by having godly children—or raising up spiritual children—and not ending up in divorce court. Family is a great calling and a high purpose, and God wants you both to never forget it.

My Prayer to God

Lord, I pray You would help both my husband and me to remember that the purpose of our marriage, and any children we may have, is to glorify You. I know we are one in Your sight, but help us to truly become one in our hearts toward each other. Help us not to live in separate worlds, but to grow closer together with each passing year. Where we have already grown apart, I pray You would stop that drift between us and reverse our course so we are headed in the same direction.

Teach us how to glorify You in the way we treat each other and in the way we raise our children—or raise up spiritual children—to follow You. Help us to "take heed" to our spirit so that we are always controlled by *Your* Spirit and no other. Even though I know that the purpose of our marriage and our family is always to glorify You, I know we cannot do that without Your help. Enable each of us to rise above our own selfishness and put renewed desire in our hearts to serve You only.

In Jesus' name I pray.

46

When I Have Wrong Thoughts

That you put off,
concerning your former conduct,
the old man which grows corrupt
according to the deceitful lusts,
and be renewed in the spirit of your mind.

EPHESIANS 4:22-23

WE WOMEN CAN SOMETIMES imagine a romantic moment or encounter, which isn't a problem unless we are imagining it with someone other than our husband. It's possible that we can be somewhere and see someone, either in person or in an image of some kind, and think a lustful thought. We can also think other kinds of thoughts—critical, fearful, or negative thoughts—thoughts that are not right and do us no good. That's why we have to keep a close guard over our mind.

When thoughts that are not of the Lord enter your mind,

you must reject them. When negative thinking begins to play over and over, you have to put a stop to it. You must stand strong against any lie of the enemy that is a setup for your demise. You must tear out, put off, and throw away from you any thinking that takes you away from the will of God and closer to the enemy's plans for your life (Matthew 5:29).

You have been given control over your mind, so you can choose to either fill it with the things of God or let whatever comes into it reside there. It's not a sin that a wrong thought comes. The sin is in letting it find a home in your mind and grow into something that will eventually be tormenting. Your old self could be corrupted by "deceitful lusts." But your born-again self can choose to have a renewed mind. The minute a lustful, negative, or wrong thought enters your mind is the time to choose to live in that renewed mind. Begin by praising God that He is greater than all your fears, doubts, lusts, and tormenting thoughts. Ask Him to help you be thoroughly renewed in the spirit of your mind. He will do that.

My Prayer to God

LORD, I ask that You would fill my mind with only thoughts that please You. Where I have allowed any lustful thoughts of anyone except my husband, I confess that to You as sin. I reject them from my mind. I confess any negative thoughts filled with doubt, fear, judgment, or anxiety. Cleanse my mind and heart of them, because I don't want to open myself up to the consequences of that kind of thinking. Forgive me and free me, as only You can do.

If there are any other thoughts I have that are not glorifying to You, take them from me and help me to be renewed in the spirit of my mind. If there is a person I need to stop being around or something I need to stop looking at or reading, help me to do that too. I don't want to commit sin in my mind in any form whatsoever. If ever I entertain wrong thoughts, convict my heart so I can repent of it immediately and be released from them. Keep me from any secret thought life that takes me further from You. Enable me to stand strong against the enemy who tries to capture my thoughts. Help me to take my thoughts captive. Teach me to fill my mind with Your truth and refuse anything that is in opposition to that.

In Jesus' name I pray.

47

When He Must Find the Liberty God Has for Him

The Lord is the Spirit;
and where the Spirit of the Lord is,
there is liberty.

2 CORINTHIANS 3:17

EVERYONE NEEDS to be free of something. We all need to be free of our past, free from our sins, and free from the bondage we have because of them. We need freedom from our own limitations and from the enemy of our soul. The list is long. If nothing else, we need to be free from the notion that we don't need to be free of anything. That's because the enemy of our soul is always seeking to entice us off the path God has for us and into some trap of temptation, sin, or disobedience he has planned for us.

It is not hard for a wife to see what her husband needs to be set free of because it is usually very clear to her. The challenge is not constantly reminding him of it, but instead continually praying he will find the freedom God has for him.

It is sometimes difficult for a man to see his own need for liberation. Too often he may accept things about himself as being "just the way I am." If you see clearly something your husband needs to be free of and he doesn't, ask the Lord to reveal it to him. Ask God to open up your husband's heart to hear the truth—from the Lord, from you, or from someone else God puts in his life. Then ask God to help your husband seek the presence of the Holy Spirit—who is the Spirit of liberty—where all freedom is found. That may seem like an impossible prayer to have answered, but nothing is too hard for God.

My Prayer to God

Lord, I am grateful that You are the Spirit of liberty and in Your presence we find freedom from whatever keeps us from becoming all You made us to be. I pray my husband will find freedom from anything that keeps him from moving into all You have for him. Enable him to understand that in Your presence he can find freedom from anything that controls him other than You. Liberate him from whatever limits him and keeps him from living Your way and doing what You have called him to do.

Deliver my husband from any wrong mind-sets, bad attitudes, negative thoughts, or unwise actions. Release him from all addictions, enticements, temptations, harmful habits, or pollution of the mind and soul. Liberate him from destructive memories of past events. Where something has taken hold of his mind or heart that is not of You, I pray You would open his eyes to see the truth about it and convict him of his need to reject it. Don't let him pursue something that takes him away from Your will for his life. Give him a vision of the freedom You have for him. Enable him to see that liberty doesn't mean freedom to do whatever he wants; it means freedom from anything that keeps him from doing what *You* want. Help him find the liberty that comes from being in Your presence. I know if You set him free, Lord, he will be completely free (John 8:36).

In Jesus' name I pray.

48

When We Should Be in Agreement About Our Children

Train up a child in the way
he should go, and when he is old
he will not depart from it.

PROVERBS 22:6

SERIOUS STRIFE can happen between a husband and wife when they don't agree over the raising of their children. What seems like a good marriage can end in divorce over the continual inability to come to an agreement about how to raise a child. And that is in every way opposite of what God wants a marriage to be. There is a right way and a wrong way to raise children, and parents have to find that *together*. There are some areas where it is not necessarily an issue of right or wrong; it is a matter of agreement between the mother and father about what is best for the child. Without this agreement, however, the wrong part of it ends up being more about what the parents are doing than the child. It is always wrong when parents cannot be in unity.

As parents, the two of you must be able to talk things out away from the presence of your child or children so you can present a united front. Kids don't rule a marriage. If they do, then that marriage is upside down from where it should be. A marriage is supposed to provide security—a safe place for children to grow. Boundaries for children are set by parents in agreement with each other. You cannot raise up a child in the way he should go if you are sending mixed messages about what that way is.

Don't allow your children to keep you in disunity. Decide who the adults in the family are, and who are the children, and then act accordingly. Pray for the adults to be more mature than the children. Ask God to help you both be in agreement about all aspects of parenting. If child-raising issues are not worked out, there will be irreparable repercussions for years to come.

My Prayer to God

LORD, I pray You would help my husband and me to be in total agreement with regard to raising our children. Where we have disagreed in the past, enable us to come into complete unity now. If this disunity has caused problems for our children or unresolved strife between the two of us, I confess that before You as sin and ask that You would bring restoration to our entire family. Enable us to see things from Your perspective. Where one of us is completely wrong, I pray You would open that person's eyes to the truth. Where our disagreement has been over an issue that is neither right nor wrong according to Your Word, help us to work together to see each other's side and come to some workable solution.

Pour out Your Spirit on my husband and me, and guide us in every decision we make as parents. Give us Your wisdom. Dissolve every impasse. Lead us to make the right conclusions so that we agree on what Your will is concerning each child. We release our children into Your hands, trusting You to help us raise them solidly up in Your ways so that they will not depart from them when they are grown. Grow us up too, so that we are mature enough to be in complete agreement at all times—especially when raising our children.

In Jesus' name I pray.

49

When I Need to Build Him Up

Comfort each other and edify one another.

1 THESSALONIANS 5:11

HOW MANY MARRIAGES break up because one person in the marriage was repeatedly made to feel bad about themselves and just couldn't continue to live with it any longer? There are enough things that happen in life to destroy our sense of self-worth. We don't need it coming from our spouse, who is supposed to be our greatest source of support. The Bible says that God's Word is able to build us up (Acts 20:32). It also says that you can build yourselves up in faith, praying in the Holy Spirit (Jude 1:20). So our true source of edification and being built up comes from a relationship with the Lord. But as husband and wife, we also must hear encouragement from each other.

Ask God what you can say or do to build up your husband.

You may be thinking, *What is he doing to build me up?* But you can't let yourself go there. If you feel your husband doesn't do enough for you in the way of encouraging or comforting, tell the Lord how it makes you feel. Ask Him to convict your husband's heart about that. Then pray for healing of your own heart.

In spite of whether your husband has built you up or not, deliberately commend him for something good and right he has done. Thank him for what you appreciate about him. If you have trouble doing that, ask God to help you obey Him by giving comfort and edification to your husband. You may find that God is healing and building up your own heart as you do.

My Prayer to God

Lord, show me how to build my husband up in a good and positive way. Reveal to me any areas where he is feeling insecure or inadequate so that I can reassure him of his value. Where he is discouraged, help me to remind him of his accomplishments, abilities, and skills. Help me to encourage him regarding his gifts and calling. Where I am not seeing them clearly myself, reveal to me all that You have put in him so that I can point those things out and help him see them too. Show me ways to build up his confidence, not just in himself, but in Your ability to work powerfully in him.

Where I have in any way contributed to his feeling bad about himself, no matter how innocently, I repent of that. Help me to make up for it and undo any damage it has caused. If I have manifested unforgiveness or resentment, I confess that before You and ask You to help me forgive him for anything I have held against him. Where I have not shown respect for him because of something he has done, or *not* done, restore that esteem in me for him again. He is Your child, just as I am. Help me to always see him as that, and build him up just as You would have me to do. Enable him to do the same for me. I pray You will help us both "pursue the things which make for peace and the things by which one may edify another" (Romans 14:19).

In Jesus' name I pray.

50

When He Has Done Something That Is Hard to Forgive

Judge not, and you shall not be judged.
Condemn not, and you shall not be condemned.
Forgive, and you will be forgiven.

LUKE 6:37

COMPLETE FORGIVENESS is often a work in progress. It shouldn't be like that, because unforgiveness is never God's perfect will for us. He wants us to forgive everything completely and immediately. After all, that's what He has done for us. But *He* is *God* and *we* are *not*. We can't always do things perfectly—at least not without His help—and He knows that. So He helps us to forgive. And forgiveness is crucial in a marriage.

We've all heard the horrible stories—and perhaps we have lived through some of them ourselves—of how a husband broke his wife's heart and destroyed their marriage. And it's not just about infidelity. It can be other things, such as deception, lying, financial irresponsibility, drinking, gambling, drug abuse, cruelty, carelessness in raising the children, betrayal, verbal abuse, or even something as serious as physical abuse. These are big issues that destroy trust, desire, joy, hope, and enthusiasm for life. If anything like that has happened to you, the first step toward healing is forgiveness. That does not mean you have to sit there and take it. No abuse should be tolerated for even *one* moment. If you are in *any* kind of danger, ask God to help you remove yourself from the abuser and forgive from afar. Abuse is demonic at its source, and it does not get better on its own. It goes against everything God is and what He has for you, and there is no excuse for it. Don't tolerate it, but get help. Don't deal with this alone.

If your husband has done something you find hard to forgive—it doesn't have to be anything as bad as what was mentioned above—ask God to help you. He will. *Remember that forgiving him doesn't make him right; it makes you free.* And you need that freedom from unforgiveness in order to live in peace. Only God can help you forgive the unforgiveable.

My Prayer to God

LORD, I need Your help in order to forgive my husband completely. I don't feel like forgiving him for certain things, but I know forgiveness is a choice. And I know that to choose to do anything other than forgive is a dead-end street, and I won't be able to get beyond it until I turn and repent. Help me to do that so I can move on with my life.

I pray specifically about the thing that upsets me most right now that my husband has done or said. If I am not seeing this situation clearly, show me the truth. Or if I have in any way been partly to blame for this happening, show me what I need to do to bring healing. But if he has done wrong, I pray You would convict his heart about it and draw him to You to make things right. Give him no peace until he repents of what he did and seeks You and Your restoration. When he has found freedom from condemnation before You, help me not to continue to condemn him. Help me to forgive him completely, just as You have forgiven me. Help us both to learn from this entire situation.

In Jesus' name I pray.

51

When We Need Financial Wisdom

The blessing of the Lord makes one rich,
and He adds no sorrow with it.

PROVERBS 10:22

GOD PROMISES to "supply all your need according to His riches in glory by Christ Jesus" when you love and serve Him (Philippians 4:19). But that doesn't mean every day, all the time. Sometimes He uses financial need to test us, train us, or teach us. Sometimes He wants us to obey Him by giving more (Proverbs 28:27). Or He wants us to seek Him and trust Him for all our financial blessings (Luke 12:29-31). Other times He is leading us to do something different in our lives, and this is the way He gets our attention so we will follow Him (Psalm 34:10). God always wants us to seek Him first before anything else, because when we do that we will receive all we need (Luke 12:31).

When you pray for financial blessings, ask God to show you whatever you need to see about your finances. Are you experiencing a financial shortfall? Is one about to happen? Do you need to cut expenses? Live a simpler and less expensive lifestyle? Sell something? Change your job? Be wiser in your financial decisions? Give more to Him and to others? Or simply seek Him first for everything and learn to depend on Him for all you need?

David said that he had never seen "the righteous forsaken, nor his descendents begging bread" (Psalm 37:25). He said that "those who seek the Lord shall not lack any good thing" (Psalm 34:10). Let those words be a great encouragement to you. Live God's way, seek Him for wisdom to guide you in all financial matters, and pray that His financial blessings will bring no sorrow with them.

My Prayer to God

Lord, I come to You with thanksgiving for all You have given us, and how You have blessed and sustained us for all this time. I lift up to You our finances and thank You for Your Word that promises You will supply all our needs (Philippians 4:19). I pray You would bless us with Your provision now. Open the storehouse of heaven and pour financial blessings upon us. Give us wisdom as to how to handle all finances, and keep us from making any foolish decisions. Bless our work with success.

Reveal to us how we can earn more and handle our finances more efficiently. Show us where we have spent unwisely and how we can cut back expenses. Show us if we are doing what You want us to do, or if You have other work for us. Open our eyes to see where we are not living Your way with regard to our finances. Convict us if we need to give more to You and to others. Teach us how to save, spend, invest, and better organize our money. I know that our true treasure is found in You. Forgive us for any times when we have not fully lived out that truth. We choose to seek You and Your kingdom first in our lives, trusting that You will provide all we need.

In Jesus' name I pray.

52

When I Want the Inward Renewal Only God Can Give

We do not lose heart. Even though
our outward man is perishing,
yet the inward man is being
renewed day by day.

2 CORINTHIANS 4:16

ONE OF THE GREATEST THINGS about walking with the Lord is that even as you are growing older, inwardly you are being renewed every day. What wonderful hope there is in that for us all, because even on the days when we feel tired, sick, beaten down, creaky, old, or as though we are rapidly deteriorating, we can trust that because we are walking with God, we are being renewed daily in our spirit and soul.

How many times have we wives not been pleasant to be around—or at the very least, ungracious—all because we don't feel well or do not feel good about ourselves in some way? Even if we *think* we *look* old and tired, it can make us less than uplifting to be close to. And we can feel old and tired even when we're not actually either of those things. But one of the ways we can combat that is to find renewal in the Lord. He works that in us when we stay close to Him.

Getting old is a fact of life, but being rejuvenated in your mind, soul, and spirit is a promise of God. And it is not something you have to strive or strain to make happen. It happens automatically when you are in the Lord's presence. As you pray and speak words to Him of worship and praise, He fills you afresh with His Spirit. And with His Spirit always comes freedom from stress and anguish, and release from self-doubt and fear. In His presence you find refreshment, rejuvenation, and restoration. Ask Him to renew you in every possible way today. He will do that. And that is no small thing, especially as the years go by.

My Prayer to God

LORD, how I thank You that even though I am growing older every year, because I walk with You I am being renewed every day. Help me to not worry about the time to come, because my future is in Your hands. Help me rejoice in each day and every birthday, because it means I am becoming more enriched in my soul and spirit because of Your Spirit in me. I pray You would enable me to remain attractive to my husband. As we both grow older, help us to always see the best in each other. I pray that as I age, the beauty of Your Spirit will become increasingly attractive to him and to others. Enable me to remain young in heart, soul, and mind. I pray that my ever-renewing vitality will be something that causes him to feel younger as well.

Teach me to look to Your Word as a well from which I can draw a life-sustaining flow of Your Spirit. Whenever I look in the mirror and am less than pleased with my reflection, help me to not dwell on that, but rather to look deeper into my soul to see the beauty of *Your reflection* there. I pray Your joy and peace in me will add light to my countenance and be something my husband and others recognize as coming from Your Spirit in me. Renew me again today and every day so that I will rejoice in each new year as a testimony to Your goodness.

In Jesus' name I pray.

53

When He Has Unrest in His Mind

Though we walk in the flesh, we do not war according to the flesh. For the weapons of our warfare are not carnal but mighty in God for pulling down strongholds, casting down arguments and every high thing that exalts itself against the knowledge of God, bringing every thought into captivity to the obedience of Christ.

2 Corinthians 10:3-5

EVERYONE CAN HAVE unrest in their mind at some time. It's part of the enemy's plan to torment us. Mental unrest will happen when we are living in a way that is opposed to God's ways and laws. But it can also happen when we are doing something right, such as moving out into ministry, or into the will of God and *away* from the enemy's plan for our life. Being aware of the source of any mental unrest is important to getting rid of it.

If you are not sure if your husband experiences any unrest in his mind, ask him. Men don't often share these things unless asked. Sometimes not even then. If he doesn't share anything, ask God to reveal to you whatever you need to see. He will show you. Does your husband have trouble sleeping because he's thinking too much? Is he unable to shut off his mind? Does he overthink everything? If your husband is not walking with the Lord, that is the first thing to address in prayer. But even if your husband doesn't know the Lord, you can still pray about this. A nonbelieving husband can be set free from that mental torment when his believing wife consistently prays for him.

If mental unrest becomes an ongoing struggle that interferes with the quality of your husband's life, it is a stronghold that needs to be broken. Speak the Word of God over him—not as a lecture but as a declaration of truth *for him*. Declare that God has given him nothing less than a sound mind (2 Timothy 1:7). Pray that he will "bring every thought into captivity" in obedience to the Lord. Mental unrest has no power in light of the truth, and it need not have any part in our lives.

My Prayer to God

Lord, I pray for my husband to be released from any disturbing thoughts in his mind. Set him free from all unreasonable fear, and liberate him from every lie of the enemy. Enable him to see the enemy's lies for what they are, and give him the strength to refuse to entertain them. Help him to recognize enemy encroachment on his mind when it happens. Teach him that he doesn't war in the flesh against the enemy, but in the Spirit. Help him to cast down every argument against You in his mind. Strengthen him to reject anything that exalts itself against the knowledge of You. Teach him to bring "every thought into captivity to the obedience of Christ" (2 Corinthians 10:3-5). Take away all mental unrest from him and give him Your peace.

Show me anything I need to see so that I can pray specifically. Help us both to see the truth in Your Word that sets us free. I declare on his behalf that You have given him a sound mind (2 Timothy 1:7). Give him faith to believe that. Enable him to face his thoughts armed with Your Word and Your power, and to refuse to allow them to control his mind and his life. Open his eyes to see You as his deliverer.

In Jesus' name I pray.

54

When We Need a New Perspective

You, brethren, have been called to liberty;
only do not use liberty as an opportunity for the flesh,
but through love serve one another.

GALATIANS 5:13

AS WE GROW in the liberty God gives us, we also find freedom to stop thinking about ourselves all the time. When we are in the flesh, we dwell on what *we* need and want and must have in order to be happy. But freedom from self-focus liberates us to serve one another. God says we must think of others first—and most importantly our *significant other*—and we must serve him. That doesn't mean becoming a slave who is taken for granted, mistreated, not allowed freedom, and not given value and equality as a person. Serving one another is an attitude of the heart that comes from seeing our lives from God's perspective.

If either you or your husband needs a new perspective in order to see things God's way, then that is something worth praying about. Ask God to give both of you new insight and the ability to see everything—especially your lives together—from *His* perspective.

Ask God to show you how to serve each other in a way that blesses and strengthens you both. Serving is something you *give* in a marriage, not something that is demanded from you. If it is demanded from you, that's slavery. Even God doesn't demand that we serve Him. He wants us to *offer* ourselves to Him. The same is true in a marriage. Willingly serving each other is a setup for God's greatest blessing in your lives. And it is probably the hardest thing to do consistently well. That's why you must pray for a new perspective to happen in each of your hearts.

My Prayer to God

LORD, I thank You for the liberty we have in You. Thank You for how You have set my husband and me free from our past and ourselves. Continue to liberate us. Help us to be rid of any wrong thinking and blindness. Help us to see things from Your perspective—especially the way we treat each other. Keep us from becoming selfish in the freedom we have in You.

I know You are continually setting us free to better serve You and others, and especially to serve each other. Help us to do that well. Give us a new perspective in our hearts and minds, because our natural tendency is to be self-focused and self-centered to the point that we neglect each other. Teach us how to bless each other in the way we act and speak. The proper attitude of heart and mind can only fully come from You. Fill us both with Your love, peace, humility, and mercy. Enable us to always act and react out of those good qualities. Lift us above our private concerns, and help us not to keep score over what one of us owes the other. Help each of us to make a greater effort—beyond what we have done in the past—to give of ourselves to each other. Give us Your perspective on our marriage relationship, and enable us to understand what we need to do to make it great.

In Jesus' name I pray.

55

When I Must Apologize

If you bring your gift to the altar,
and there remember that your brother
has something against you, leave your gift there
before the altar, and go your way.
First be reconciled to your brother, and
then come and offer your gift.

MATTHEW 5:23-24

JESUS MAKES IT CRYSTAL CLEAR that if you need to apologize to someone for something, you had better get it done right away. That's because you must be able to say "I'm sorry," "Forgive me," and "I apologize" *before* you come to the Lord with your offering of worship. God will not receive your worship of Him until you have first apologized to your husband for whatever is needed and made the way for reconciliation to come between the two of you. This is a serious requirement. If God doesn't want to hear your worship until you have apologized to whomever you need to, then you must do it now to avoid separation of any kind between you and the Lord.

Usually you know if you need to apologize to your husband for something because you feel guilty about what you have said or done—or *not* said or done. If you have trouble apologizing because doing so feels awkward, it's probably because of pride. You're embarrassed, you don't like to admit you're wrong, or you don't want your husband to gloat. But if you think of it in terms of what the *Lord expects* from you, saying you're sorry becomes easier because you want to obey *Him*. Again, you definitely don't want any barrier to come between you and the Lord.

Ask God to show you clearly if there is some reason you need to apologize to your husband. If the Lord reveals something, don't waste any time in apologizing. You'll be amazed how a simple thing like this can make an enormous difference in your marriage relationship, as well as in your relationship with God. It will open up your time of worship in the Lord's presence, and that will make room for the healing, wholeness, and blessing you need personally, as well as in your marriage.

My Prayer to God

Lord, I pray You will show me whenever I need to apologize to my husband for anything. Open my eyes to see where I have been insensitive, dismissive, uninterested, or uncaring in my words or actions. Take away any pride in me that would cause me to hesitate to apologize, because then I would have to admit I was wrong about something. Take away all pettiness from me because I want to live Your way. I don't want to give You any reason to wait to hear my offering of worship (Matthew 5:23-24). I also don't want my husband to have anything against me that stirs up feelings of hurt or resentment, or causes him to withdraw from me for any reason.

Give me the desire to do what's right. Help me to quickly say "I'm sorry" for anything I have done wrong so that we can be reconciled and all uneasy feelings between us can be dissolved. Enable me to have a right spirit so that I don't do anything I need to apologize for in the future. I pray that my actions, thoughts, and words will be pleasing to You, and my offering of worship will always be acceptable in Your sight.

In Jesus' name I pray.

56

When He Needs to Be Selfless

Let nothing be done
through selfish ambition or conceit,
but in lowliness of mind let each
esteem others better than himself.
Let each of you look out
not only for his own interests,
but also for the interests of others.

PHILIPPIANS 2:3-4

WE CAN ALL BE SELFISH from time to time, but when you believe selfishness is your husband's standard mode of operation, that is definitely something to pray about. God's Word says that *nothing* should be done out of selfish ambition or conceit. In a marriage, how can we be sure we will do that unless God enables us? What God wants is that both people in a marriage esteem their spouse more than themselves. But how well can this work in a marriage if only one person is selfless? It takes two. Both of you have to be looking out for each other's interests and not just your own.

If you believe your husband is selfish, you have to decide that no matter what he does, you will do what is right. You will be unselfish toward him. Ask God to help you with that. But pray for your husband to do that as well. It may seem selfish to you to be praying that your husband think more of you than he does of himself, but it's not. It is God's will for his life. It is to his advantage that he does so. And besides, God is requiring the same of you.

Looking out for each other like this promises the greatest success in your marriage, but it only *truly* works when you *both* are taking this step of obedience. This can be nearly impossible without God's help—because we all have a tendency toward self-focus—but it is well worth the effort to seek God's enablement. It will do wonders for your marriage.

My Prayer to God

LORD, I pray You would enable my husband to do nothing through selfish ambition or conceit, but rather to be humble and esteem others in higher regard than himself. I pray the same for myself, as well. Help us especially to relate that way toward each other. Give him a heart to always look out for me. Help me to do the same for him. Take away any selfishness in our hearts that would cause us to neglect each other in that way. Take away any conceit in us that would motivate us to keep score and think *I deserve better*. Enable us to be more like You, Jesus, who laid down Your life for us. Teach us to lay down our lives for You and serve You in our marriage by serving each other.

I know that when my husband and I live the way You want us to, we will be walking in Your perfect will. But I also know what we are made of, and even though we try, we too often fail. Only by the miracle-working power of Your Spirit enabling us can this be walked out in our lives. You have already convicted me of the need for selflessness in our marriage. I pray You would convict my husband of that as well, and enable him to do it.

In Jesus' name I pray.

57

When We Seek God's Provision

Abraham lifted his eyes and looked, and there behind him was a ram caught in a thicket by its horns. So Abraham went and took the ram, and offered it up for a burnt offering instead of his son. And Abraham called the name of the place, The-Lord-Will-Provide; as it is said to this day, "In the Mount of the Lord it shall be provided."

GENESIS 22:13-14

WHEN ABRAHAM OBEYED GOD and took his only son, Isaac, to Mount Moriah to offer him to the Lord as a burnt offering, he trusted that God would provide another offering. But if He didn't, Abraham was willing to sacrifice his only son. He did not withhold his most valuable possession from God. Even though Abraham and Sarah had waited so long to have their only son, he was willing to give that dream to God. And because of that, God promised to provide bountifully for him.

God promises to provide for us too, but He wants us to give Him our all and not put anything else before Him. We have to be willing to let go of everything—even our dreams. If you are in special need of provision right now, ask God if there is anything you need to submit to Him and release into His hands. This doesn't mean you will have to give your house away, destroy your business, or give up your children for adoption. It means surrendering all of that to God and not putting anything before Him. Dedicate your children to the Lord, and pray that He will use them for His plans. Dedicate your house to God, and ask Him to use it for His purposes. Dedicate your work or business and all you have to your heavenly Father, and ask Him to show you how to use it all for His glory. When you want provision, surrender all you have to God, and see how He blesses you with all that you need and more.

My Prayer to God

LORD, I come to You with the need my husband and I have for Your provision. I thank You that You are the Lord who provides (Genesis 22:14). Show us what we can do to further open up the flow of Your abundance in our lives. Or show us what we should or should *not* do to keep from stopping up the flow of all you have for us. Not that we can ever do anything to deserve Your blessing, but I know there are things we *can* do that will keep us from being a hindrance to all You want to bring into our lives.

On behalf of my husband, I surrender all that we have to You. We release from our hands to Yours the things and people we have held too tightly. I dedicate our lives to Your purpose and glory. Show us whatever You want us to let go of, and help us to do that. Everything we have been clinging to, we release into Your hands. We thank You for all You have given us, for we know that everything we have comes from You. I praise You as our loving, heavenly Father, who provides for all our needs. Thank You in advance for Your wonderful provision to us.

In Jesus' name I pray.

58

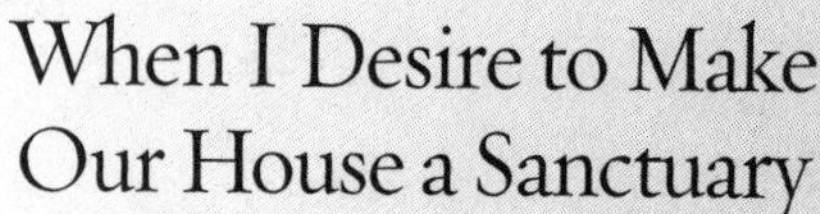

When I Desire to Make Our House a Sanctuary

Through wisdom a house is built,
and by understanding it is established;
by knowledge the rooms are filled
with all precious and pleasant riches.

PROVERBS 24:3-4

WE'VE ALL SEEN beautifully decorated houses that seem cold when we are in them. We've also seen simple and humbly put together homes that are so warm and inviting we don't want to leave. But this is not a case against beautifully decorated homes, because we've also all seen just the opposite—a beautifully decorated home that is warm and inviting, or a humble home that is quite cold and uninviting. It is not the decoration or size that determines whether your house becomes a sanctuary or a refuge; it is the spirit that resides there. And people can sense that spirit when they walk in the door, whether they know what it is or not.

Invite the presence of God to reside in your home. Ask God to help you arrange your home in a way that is a comfort and blessing to the people who live there, as well as those who visit. Ask Him to give you the wisdom, understanding, and knowledge that come only from Him in order to accomplish it.

The "precious and pleasant riches" that make a house a refuge for you and your husband are the peace, love, and joy that are the rejuvenating qualities only God can bring—in other words, the presence of God. Invite God to provide the precious and pleasant riches of His Holy Spirit so He can decorate your home with the beauty of His presence. It will be a sanctuary in which personal revival will happen daily.

My Prayer to God

LORD, I invite You to inhabit our home. Fill it with Your Spirit of love, peace, and joy, so much so that it affects my husband and me in a powerful way whenever we are there. Help me to do what it takes to make our home a sanctuary, for us and for whoever spends time in it. Show me how to create a refuge that is warm, inviting, orderly, and strife-free. Give me a vision of what needs to be done, changed, or enhanced in order to make it more inviting. I pray that our home will be a place we always want to be. May it be so rejuvenating that it gives us strength and health just to be there.

I invite Your presence to dwell in our home so that we both sense Your comfort, calm, and beauty every time we walk through the door. Take away any tension or coldness we have brought into it. Surround our home with Your protection so that no harm comes to it or anyone inside it. Keep us safe from all intruders and dangers. I pray that no fire, storm, earthquake, or any other disaster will ever damage or destroy it. Enable both of us to care diligently for the home You have provided for us. I pray we will never allow in anything that is not in keeping with Your ways and Your will. Fill our home with the "precious and pleasant riches" of Your Spirit and the beauty and comfort of Your presence.

In Jesus' name I pray.

59

When He Needs to Put Away All Anger

Let all bitterness, wrath, anger, clamor,
and evil speaking be put away
from you, with all malice.

EPHESIANS 4:31

IF THERE IS ONE difficult situation I hear about most from wives—other than the way-too-common sin of infidelity—it is about husbands with an anger problem. And this is a problem of major proportions. I don't know any wife who handles a husband's frequent anger well, especially when it is directed at her. Many women endure it because of God's grace, but it is a constant source of pain. And it too often becomes so unbearable that divorce seems a welcome relief. When a wife feels her own survival is at stake, then separation and divorce are an automatic reaction for self-preservation.

God's Word tells every husband to treat his wife with understanding and honor, and to be considerate of her vulnerability and delicacy, so that his prayers will not be hindered (1 Peter 3:7). I have never seen a man who verbally or physically abused his wife who continued to have success in his life. This same verse also says that a husband and wife are "heirs *together*" (emphasis added) of all God has for them. So if a husband refuses to treat his wife well and instead vents his anger on her, *he* will not inherit the blessings God has for them both, and his prayers will not be answered.

If you are too often the object of your husband's anger, and it has become emotionally or physically depleting for you, seek God about finding help for this situation. The Bible says, "The discretion of a man makes him slow to anger, and his glory is to overlook a transgression" (Proverbs 19:11). It also says to "cease from anger, and forsake wrath" (Psalm 37:8). That means he has a choice about whether to vent his anger or not. Pray that your husband will make the right choice because the consequences for not doing so are severe. If you are one of the blessed few who has a husband who never vents anger, thank God for that and pray he will always be that way.

My Prayer to God

Lord, I pray You would take all anger away from my husband. His angry displays can only cause harm to himself, to me, to our children, and to others around him. Teach him Your ways and enable him to understand that nothing good ever comes from venting anger on others—especially his wife or children. Enable him to see what strife it causes in our marriage and our family (Proverbs 29:22). Give him the wisdom to recognize that anger is in the heart of fools (Ecclesiastes 7:9). Take away any angry spirit, for I know that frequent anger directed at a spouse is a fruit of the flesh and it never pleases You (Romans 8:6-8). It only causes trouble for his own soul (Proverbs 11:17).

Fill him with Your love and take away any need to gratify his own flesh by giving free reign to wrath. Strengthen him to control it and to give no place to it in his mind. I pray You will help me avoid words that stir up his anger (Proverbs 15:1). Enable me to do nothing to provoke it. Open his eyes to see this unreasonable character flaw and enable him to make the decision to put away all anger from his life. Thank You, Lord, for helping him refuse to give place to anger.

In Jesus' name I pray.

60

When We Must Send Our Children the Right Message

When your son asks you in time to come,
saying, "What is the meaning of
the testimonies, the statutes, and the
judgments which the Lord our God
has commanded you?" then you shall say
to your son: "We were slaves of
Pharaoh in Egypt, and the Lord brought
us out of Egypt with a mighty hand."

DEUTERONOMY 6:20-21

TIME AND AGAIN God's Word instructs us to tell our children about the Lord—who He is and what He has done for us. We must tell them what the Bible says and how it has changed us. We are to share with them what the Lord has specifically done in our lives—how we were once slaves to our own wants, but now God has set us free and brought us out of the snares of the world and into His kingdom.

It is most important that you and your husband be sending the same message about the Lord to your children. That's why you need to ask God to help you communicate His truth to your children in a way that they can comprehend—whether they are young children, or adults, or somewhere in between. Too often we become busy and assume our children are picking all this up by osmosis. But unless you are specifically instructing them, they may be picking up *other* things by osmosis that you don't want them to absorb.

Too much of the world can creep into your children's minds, souls, and spirits every day without your even realizing it. They need that double-barrel message from the two of you to have a double-strong impact. If your husband is not yet a believer, pray that he will at least not object to your teaching your children about the Lord. Even if you have only known the Lord a short time yourself, you already have too much knowledge to not share what you know. Whatever the situation, pray that you and your husband will always send your children the right message.

My Prayer to God

LORD, I pray You would enable my husband and me to be in complete agreement about the way we communicate to our children the truth of who You are and what You have done for us. Help us to speak clearly with them about how You rescued us from the emptiness and futility of life apart from You. Help us to live Your way so they can see it. Enable us to be in unity about what we believe. Where my husband doesn't believe exactly as I do, I pray You would open his eyes to see the truth. Bring revelation and light to whichever one of us is ignorant about Your ways. I pray there will be no strife or argument between us over this, but that we will work this out together.

Give us both the motivation and desire to talk to our children, no matter what age they are—even if they are grown now—in order to share the goodness of walking with You. I know we don't have to be Bible scholars in order to share the good news in Your Word, but we do have to take the time to do it. Help us to communicate to our children the love we have for You in a way that draws them toward You. Help us to communicate our love and Your love for *them* in a way that heals and attracts them to Jesus.

In Jesus' name I pray.

61

When I Need to Sense His Love for Me

Husbands, love your wives, just as Christ also loved the church and gave Himself for her...So husbands ought to love their own wives as their own bodies; he who loves his wife loves himself. For no one ever hated his own flesh, but nourishes and cherishes it, just as the Lord does the church.

EPHESIANS 5:25,28-29

IF YOU HAVE ALWAYS FELT loved by your husband, thank God for that and pray it will always be that way. However, if you are like many wives who don't *feel* truly loved by their husband, you can pray for that to change. While you cannot make someone love you if they won't, you *can* pray for your husband to do God's will and learn how to show his love in ways that are meaningful to you. Love is a language, and some men don't speak it well enough. If your husband seems distant, preoccupied, or unaffectionate, God can teach him to be more like *Him*, and He is the absolute king of the love language.

The Bible says a husband is supposed to love his wife as he loves himself. He is also to love his wife the way Jesus loves His believers. Jesus gave His life as the ultimate sacrifice. This seems like an impossibly high standard for a husband to live up to, but one of the ways a husband sacrifices his life for his wife is by openly showing his love for her.

Every woman needs to feel loved by her husband. And you can pray for that, because it is God's will that every husband love his wife as he loves himself. If love has been covered over in your husband's heart, pray that God will uncover it and bring it to the light. If love has died between you, ask God to resurrect it. He is an expert at doing that—and He can accomplish it in even the hardest of hearts.

My Prayer to God

LORD, help me to fulfill Your commandment to love my husband as myself (John 13:34). I pray You would enable my husband to love me in that same way. Teach him to show his love for me in ways I can perceive. Open my eyes to see the ways he already shows his love for me that perhaps I am not appreciating. Although You require him to love me as he loves himself, I don't want to pressure him to do more than he can at this time. But I do want him to live Your way so that he can receive the blessings You have for him.

Enable my husband to open up to Your love for him so that he can better express his love for me. Where love has waned or even died between us, rekindle it in each of our hearts. If unforgiveness in either of us has been a destroyer of love, I pray You would help us to forgive each other completely so that our prayers are not hindered and Your love can flow freely between us again. Where I have been neglectful of him, or not been affectionate enough, or not shown love to him the way I should, help me to change that. Only You, the God of love, can teach us how to love each other the way that You love us.

In Jesus' name I pray.

62

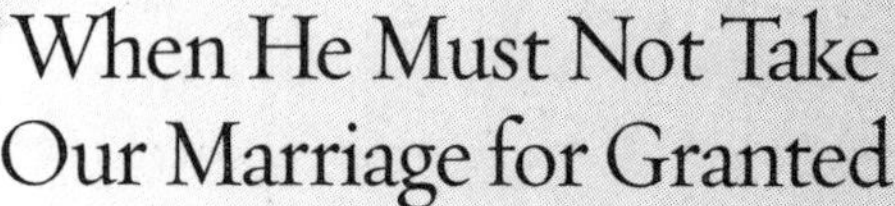

When He Must Not Take Our Marriage for Granted

Let him who thinks he stands
take heed lest he fall.

1 Corinthians 10:12

WHEN YOU ARE WORKING HARD to establish your business or career, or you are consumed with raising children or with other interests, it's easy to devote far more time to that than to your marriage. And when things are going well between you and your husband, you can mistakenly believe they always will and so you don't have to try as hard as you used to. But every marriage takes a deliberate effort by both people in it in order to see that the other person feels loved, cared for, valued, respected, and understood. You cannot go about doing what you do day after day and expect that to just happen. It doesn't. You have to make an effort to not take your marriage for granted.

You are probably already thinking along these lines or you wouldn't be reading this book. It's more likely that you are concerned about your husband taking *you* for granted and not putting enough effort into your marriage. If so, pray that his eyes will be opened to see the truth about that. No married man should ever assume that he and his wife can never drift apart, or find other interests, or just stop loving and caring for each other. It happens all the time. On top of that, you both have the added concern of an enemy who wants your marriage destroyed, because he doesn't want anything in your life to be glorifying to God.

Besides praying for your husband to make an effort in the marriage, pray that God will show you how to convince your husband that you don't ever take him for granted. Hopefully, your actions will open his eyes and inspire him "who thinks he stands" to "take heed lest he fall."

My Prayer to God

LORD, I pray You would show my husband and me how to avoid taking each other for granted. Teach us to put a consistent effort into our marriage by extending ourselves to each other in kindness, consideration, and love. Help me to do that whether my husband extends the courtesy to me or not, but I pray You will convict *his* heart about this as well. Inspire him to communicate love, caring, understanding, and concern. Teach him to see our marriage as a gift You have given to our lives. When either of us is acting like a gift the other one would like to return, enable us to become more like You so we will have *Your* heart for each other and be the blessing to each other that we should be.

Reveal to me, even now as I am praying, what I can do

to bless my husband today. How can I show him I value who he is and what he means to my life? Break through any hardness in my heart that is resistant to doing that. Show him the same thing about me, and take away any resistance in him as well. Don't let him become so sure that our marriage will never fail that he feels he doesn't need to invest anything of himself in it. Help him to see our marriage as something to carefully protect and preserve for our pleasure and Your glory.

In Jesus' name I pray.

63

When We Need Others to Pray with Us

Again I say to you that if two of you agree on earth concerning anything that they ask, it will be done for them by My Father in heaven. For where two or three are gathered together in My name, I am there in the midst of them.

MATTHEW 18:19-20

WHEN YOUR HUSBAND'S or your needs are serious, you must take heed to these verses in Scripture and call in the troops. Pray for each of you to have two or three friends who are strong believers—people who are mature in the Lord, who understand and believe His Word, who have strong faith, and who live God's way—and cultivate reliable and solid friendships with them. Find people who will *pray with you,* and *you with them,* whenever either of you need it. Not enough can be said about the power of praying together with others. Every couple needs that, no matter who they are.

When we only pray alone, it is too easy to become discouraged if we don't see answers to our prayers. Prayer with others, however, forces us to focus on what our needs really are and to verbalize them in such a way that people understand how to pray for us. Praying together with other believers encourages us to not give up. It inspires hope and renewed faith. Another important aspect of praying together is that it helps us to form great and lasting friendships. That's because we always grow to love the people we pray for. We become very closely connected to them in a spiritual way—and they with us—and that creates a bond which is not easily broken.

Finding friends with whom you can pray when you need to is something you must pray about. Ask the Lord to lead you and your husband to at least two good, godly friends for each of you—girlfriends for you and male friends for your husband. Also ask Him to give you one or more godly couples with whom you feel comfortable going to for prayer as a foursome, as well as for companionship. Even if you see no one in your lives right now who could possibly fulfill that need, God can bring people to you who are right for both of you. The promise of His presence when two or more are gathered in His name is more than enough incentive to follow through on this.

My Prayer to God

Lord, I ask that You would help my husband and me to find two good, godly, faith-filled prayer partners and friends for each of us. I pray they would be people with whom we feel comfortable going to for prayer when we need to. Lead us to men and women who live by Your Word and believe in the power of prayer in Your name. I also pray You would bring one or more married couples into our lives with whom we can find unity in regard to our beliefs and faith. May they be people with whom we can establish deep and lasting friendships that are edifying and uplifting.

Where there are friends in either of our lives who are not good influences or who lead us away from Your will or Your ways, take them out of our lives in order to make room for those with whom You would have us to spend our time. I pray You will be the center of all our friendships, and that prayer will be the glue that cements these relationships together. Your Word says, "He who walks with wise men will be wise, but the companion of fools will be destroyed" (Proverbs 13:20). I pray neither of us will be destroyed because we failed to seek out people with godly wisdom with whom we can pray.

In Jesus' name I pray.

64

When I Don't Want to Nag

The contentions of a wife are a continual dripping.

PROVERBS 19:13

WHEN A WIFE SEES something wrong with what her husband does or says, she wants to help him fix it. This works well only if he can see it too and *wants* her to help him fix it. However, if he cannot see the problem, or doesn't think what he is doing is that big of an issue, then he believes she is being unfairly critical. If his ego is such that he is resistant to doing anything his wife wants him to (certain men are that way, you know), then a wife has to be very careful that even polite suggestions don't become perceived as nagging.

Nagging is so easy to do. You see the problem, you have the solution, and you frequently remind your husband of it. But if you don't want to become a "continual dripping"—in other words, a constant irritation—you must not be relentless in contending for something, no matter how passionate you are about it. It is far better to speak your concerns to God *before* you speak to your husband about them. That way God can give you a more pleasant approach and a sense of timing, and at the same time prepare your husband's heart to receive what you have to say.

If you have already voiced your concerns about a specific issue to your husband many times and it is bordering on nagging, then take those concerns to God, release them into His hands, and ask Him to speak to your husband about it. You will be amazed at how much more is accomplished by doing that and allowing the Holy Spirit to lead you as to what, if anything, to say or not say. There can be no happiness without peace in your home and marriage. And your prayers are crucial to preserving that peace.

My Prayer to God

LORD, I bring to You the concerns I have that I want my husband to hear. Show me what I should or should not say. Help me to not be rash with my words. If I need to say something, give me the words to speak. Fill my heart with Your love and kindness, and help me to choose my words carefully. Prepare his heart to receive what I have to say. I pray that whatever changes need to be made in him or in me would be accomplished by the power of Your Spirit working in us both. If I need to back off and let this go, show me that and take away this burden of concern from my mind.

If my attitude is not right before You or my husband, give me a new perspective and a change of heart. If I am supposed to be completely silent about this and pray only, help me to know that too. Take away any critical spirit I have and enable me to hold back my words to him and pray to You instead. I don't want to become a nag or cause a continual dripping of irritation to rain down upon my husband. I want to bring peace into our relationship and our home. I invite You, the Spirit of peace, to reign in my heart and in our marriage.

In Jesus' name I pray.

65

When He Needs God to Establish His Work

Let the beauty of the Lord our God be upon us,
and establish the work of our hands for us;
yes, establish the work of our hands.

PSALM 90:17

EVERY MAN NEEDS God's blessing upon his work. Whatever stage your husband is in with regard to his work—whether he is looking for a temporary job that will lead to a better one, or he is setting up his own business, or somewhere in between—he needs the favor of God upon him and what he does. He also must have a special quality that attracts people and causes them to trust him and feel comfortable around him. When the favor of the Lord is upon him, people will seek him out and be confident doing business with him. Having the hand of God establishing his work means that it will become consistent, stable, enduring, successful, and fruitful.

Your husband's success in his work affects you greatly. If things are not going well, you can both not only suffer financially but relationally as well. A man who is out of work, or whose work situation is not going well, can be very difficult to be around. If your husband has reason to be concerned about his work, pray for the specific details of what he is experiencing. If everything is going smoothly, pray that it will continue to do so.

Ask God to open doors of opportunity for your husband so that he always has good work and is not continually struggling to find it. Pray that God will establish his work perfectly, and that he will always have the favor of God as his greatest advantage.

My Prayer to God

Lord, I pray You would establish the work of my husband's hands for Your purposes. When he needs to work more diligently, I pray You would enable him to do so. When he works too hard and too long, help him to work more effectively in less time so he has proper rest. Take away any anxiety about his work so that he can have peace and joy in it. Put Your favor on him in such a way that it is noticeable to others, even if they don't understand where it comes from. I pray that people will be attracted to all of You that they see in him, and they will come to understand that You are the source of what they are attracted to.

Help my husband to always have solid and steady employment and for good pay. Give him favor with other people he works with. Enable him to establish his business so that it bears fruit for his efforts. I pray he will do such good work, and be so well appreciated for what he does, that he will always have work to do. When he becomes discouraged in his work, I pray You would give him a fresh vision. Guide him so that he doesn't make mistakes. Give him wisdom to make the right decisions. I pray he will always have Your favor upon him as a magnificent gift that opens doors and guides him through them. Enable him to accomplish far above what he has hoped. Give him fulfillment in his work and the knowledge that he is doing Your will.

In Jesus' name I pray.

66

When We Must Put a Stop to Strife

Do not grumble against one another,
brethren, lest you be condemned.
Behold, the Judge is standing at the door!

JAMES 5:9

WHAT MARRIED COUPLE has never argued? Do you know of any? Do you and your husband ever argue about anything? If so, you are not alone. In fact, you are in the majority. In a marriage where two entirely different people are becoming one—even though you are already recognized as one in the eyes of the Lord—the reality of your daily lives reveals that it is going to take some work in order to establish that oneness. It is not wrong to have a peaceful disagreement—the honest expression of each person's perspective—because you are talking things out and coming to an acceptable compromise or agreement.

However, when you have frequent arguments, strife, disagreements, and hurtful exchanges, that becomes sin in the eyes of God. And He doesn't tolerate it.

If you and your husband grumble against each other, condemnation will come from above and you will be in danger of judgment. That judgment can come in many forms, but you will know it by the misery you feel in your soul and the hurt in your heart. You will sense that you have violated the will of God for your marriage relationship and that the consequences for that are too great.

If you recognize this as a problem but are at a loss as to what to do about it, draw a line in the sand. Declare before God that you will not be a party to strife. Ask Him to put an end to strife between you and your husband the moment you begin to argue. Ask your husband to pray with you immediately about the things that are causing you stress. If he refuses to do that, then do it yourself. Your prayers are powerful enough to break that contentious spirit in both of you.

My Prayer to God

LORD, I ask that Your Spirit of peace would reign in my heart and in the heart of my husband. Whenever we have allowed arguing, grumbling, or strife to prevail between us, I confess that to You as sin. I know it does not please You, and so it is not without consequences. Where a spirit of disagreement is dominating our relationship, I ask that You would break that stronghold by the power of Your Spirit. I resist and refuse any plans of the enemy to come between us and create strife, confusion, and misunderstanding. I declare *Your* ways to be our ways.

Thank You that You have given us the mind of Christ. Thank You for giving us the Spirit of peace, unity, agreement, acceptance, and love. Pour those qualities into our hearts in greater measure than we have been open to receiving before. I pray the Judge will not have to stand at our door, because we have chosen to stop all grumbling, bickering, arguing, or fighting. Strike down any argumentative spirit in either of us so that we can always exhibit Your Spirit of patience and reason. Put an end to all strife between us.

In Jesus' name I pray.

67

When I Need to Confess My Attitude

Let us draw near with a true heart in full assurance of faith, having our hearts sprinkled from an evil conscience and our bodies washed with pure water… And let us consider one another in order to stir up love and good works.

HEBREWS 10:22,24

YOU CANNOT HAVE a close walk with God if you entertain thoughts and feelings in your heart that should be brought to God and confessed. (For example, you can't keep rehearsing over and over in your mind the things that are irritating you about your husband, and then planning a way to get even or thinking of something less than God-glorifying to say.) Because of the blood of Jesus in His victory on the cross, you can choose to walk in a new and living way that brings life. Because of His Holy Spirit in you, you can be cleansed so that your heart is right. Only when your heart is right before God are you free to view your husband in a way that stirs up love in you for him and in him for you.

You always know when your attitude is bad. You feel it heavy in your heart and mind, and eventually it manifests somewhere in your body. The good news is that you can get free of that by confessing it to God, asking Him to cleanse your mind and give you a clean heart full of love and faith. This is one of the best ways to revive a marriage. And you must make an effort to do that whenever necessary.

Even though it may feel good to hang on to a bad attitude for a while because you feel justified in having it, what you need more is to possess a heart and soul washed so clean that it can stir up something good in your marriage.

My Prayer to God

Lord, I come before You and ask that You would cleanse my attitude. "Create in me a clean heart, O God, and renew a steadfast spirit within me" (Psalm 51:10). I confess as sin any attitude I have that is not glorifying to You. Specifically I confess all thoughts about my husband that are not right in Your sight. Take every negative thought and critical attitude from me and help me to stand strong in what is true and good. I don't ever want to grieve Your Spirit or put up a wall of separation from You because of an attitude I am entertaining that is indicative of "an evil conscience."

Where my attitude has been hurtful to my husband, help

me to confess it to him in a way that is redemptive and healing. I don't want to continue on in a manner that weakens our relationship. Enable us both to have a clean heart and positive mind toward each other. Help us to forgive each other quickly and let go of grievances and anything we perceive to be offenses. Restore to us "the joy of Your salvation" and uphold us "by Your generous Spirit" (Psalm 51:12). Enable us "to stir up love and good works" toward each other.

In Jesus' name I pray.

68

When He Seeks Financial Blessings

Give, and it will be given to you:
good measure, pressed down,
shaken together, and running over
will be put into your bosom.
For with the same measure that you use,
it will be measured back to you.

LUKE 6:38

IT IS EXTREMELY IMPORTANT for you to pray about the way your husband handles finances. Ask God to keep him ethical, honest, and upright in his relationship with money. And pray he will not neglect one of the most important aspects of financial blessings, and that is giving to God. The Lord makes His thoughts on giving very clear in His Word, saying, "'Bring all the tithes into the storehouse, that there may be food in My house, and try Me now in this,' says the LORD of hosts, 'If I will not open for you the windows of heaven and pour out for you such blessing that there will not be room enough to receive it. And I will rebuke the devourer for your sakes, so that he will not destroy the fruit of your ground, nor shall the vine fail to bear fruit for you in the field,' says the LORD of hosts" (Malachi 3:10-11).

This is such an important promise. If we give to Him as He requires, He will not only pour out abundance upon us but also protect us from what could rob us of what we already have. Yet this is often hard for people to do. They have to get beyond feeling that they are giving money to a pastor, or a church, or perhaps a group of people they are not sure they trust. They have to think of it as giving to God.

If it is hard for either you or your husband to give to God, perhaps it is because you were raised with little, and it can be frightening to think about what could happen if you don't have enough. If that is the case, ask God to help you trust that He won't leave you in jeopardy. Ask Him to enable you and your husband to fearlessly obey Him in this area of your life. When you are generous toward God with all you have, God is generous toward you with all that *He* has.

My Prayer to God

LORD, I pray You would help my husband understand how to handle finances the way You have instructed in Your Word. Keep him always ethical, upright, and responsible to pay anyone to whom he owes money. Teach him to give the way You want him to—generously and without hesitation—to You and to others. Help us to tithe and give offerings to you and money to the poor. Take away any fear in either of us that says if we give to You we won't have enough for us. Help us to remember that everything we have comes from You. Thank You that when we give what You require, You will take care of all our needs.

Help us to completely trust You in every way, and especially with money. Enable my husband to always make sound financial decisions and be willing to give to You as a part of that. Help us both to be in unity about this. Teach him to find the perfect balance between overspending and being stingy. Give him the wisdom and insight to handle money sensibly. Help us to always give in a way that pleases You. Thank You for opening the windows of heaven and pouring out Your blessings upon us.

In Jesus' name I pray.

69

When We Need to Simplify Our Lives

He said to them, "Take heed and beware of covetousness, for one's life does not consist in the abundance of the things he possesses."

LUKE 12:15

WE ALL NEED TO SIMPLIFY our lives in some way, because it seems that everything in this world draws us away from "the simplicity that is in Christ" (2 Corinthians 11:3). That verse is talking about not being deceived by the enemy and corrupted away from the simplicity of the gospel of Jesus. But there is a simplicity of living when we walk with the Lord that gives us a better quality of life. If there is too much input from outside influences that intrude upon our lives, and we are not deliberately mindful of it, it can quickly become overwhelming.

One of the good things about going through a financial

crunch is that you learn where you must cut back and discover what you can live without. It forces you to sell things you don't need—or that you do need, but God helps you to live without. God wants you to find the balance between poverty and working yourself to death for material possessions (Proverbs 23:4). He can enable you to slow that runaway train of your life down and get it on the right track.

Ask God to help you and your husband become free of slavery to things and activities that take up too much of your time without adding anything of value to your life. Ask Him to show you what you can eliminate from your lives in the way of time-stealers so that you will have more time for the most important things—family and God. It is amazing how learning to live more simply takes the stress off of a marriage. You have more time to breathe, less pressure to work beyond what is good, more hours to collect your thoughts, and more time to spend with the Lord and each other.

My Prayer to God

Lord, I pray You would help my husband and me to simplify our lives so that we can be free of unnecessary stress. Give us the wisdom to get rid of things we don't need and that someone else can use. Help us to not purchase anything we can't afford and can live without. Enable us to live peaceful and quiet lives that, in their simplicity, we find to be beautiful. Help us to simplify our lifestyle, the foods we eat, the clothes we wear, the things we buy, and what we spend time on.

Teach us how to simplify the things we do and how we do them. Show us what we could eliminate of the activities and commitments we have that would free us to spend more time on the most important things—You, family, and each other. We need You to help us stop any tendency we have to allow our lives to become more and more complicated.

I pray by the power of Your Spirit that You will enable us to make our lives more manageable. When there are things that cannot be eliminated or simplified, such as the work we do for other people, I pray Your peace would reign in us to such an extent that we accomplish what is needed with less stress on our minds and bodies. May this new simplicity bring a better quality of life—a life closer to what You want for us.

In Jesus' name I pray.

70

When I Have Lost Sight of Our Future

I know the thoughts that I think toward you, says the Lord, thoughts of peace and not of evil, to give you a future and a hope.

JEREMIAH 29:11

GOD SAYS your future is good. He promises that His thoughts and plans for you are not for evil and you will always have a reason to hope. But you can lose sight of this for many different reasons, such as extended illness, chronic pain, exhaustion, being too busy to ever catch up with yourself, and, most of all, neglecting to spend regular, in-depth times with the Lord. Other things, such as disappointments, diversions, following the wrong dreams, catering to ungodly desires, allowing your thoughts to wander to unhealthy places, or receiving lies of the enemy about yourself, can all contribute to this loss of vision as well. Whatever the reason, when you lose sight of your future you also lose sight of your hope and your source of joy in life. That alone will make you depressed, anxious, apathetic, or fearful.

Even though you may think right now that this could never happen to you, the truth is that it can happen to anyone. If you have experienced any one of the situations I mentioned above, it can bring you down and cause you to lose sight of the fact that God is your future and your hope.

Whether you feel this has already happened to you, or you want to avoid it happening in the future, ask God to speak to you every day in His Word. Ask Him to meet you whenever you pray and worship Him. That is the greatest *protection from*—and *remedy for*—this ailment. The reason for that is because God is the only one who can give you a sense of your future. And that's because He *is* your future. He has planned your future and He is the key to your moving into it. Having a sense of your future doesn't necessarily mean you will know specific details, but it does mean you will have a comforting sense that you *have* a future and that it is good.

My Prayer to God

LORD, I ask that whenever I lose sight of my future, You will remind me again of all You have planned for me. The circumstances of my life sometimes cause me to doubt what's ahead, but I trust Your Word that says Your plans are to give me a future and a hope. Restore that insight to me. Renew and refresh the vision I've had at certain times. Give me a fresh, new vision I've never had before.

Where I have not spent enough time with You in prayer

and worship and reading Your Word, help me to change my habits and not let a day go by without experiencing that quality time with You. Help me to hear You speaking to my heart. When I have become too busy, or worried, or have allowed faithless thinking to dominate my mind, change my thoughts and turn them toward You. Help me to always see Your goodness in my life and never doubt it. Renew my strength, courage, and sense of direction. Enable me to understand completely that because I walk with You, I will always have a purpose and a calling. I choose to trust that Your plans for me are for good, no matter what is happening in my life.

In Jesus' name I pray.

71

When He Must Stay on the Path God Has for Him

O Lord, I know the way of man is not in himself;
it is not in man who walks to direct his own steps.

Jeremiah 10:23

We are all on a path going somewhere, but we must be certain we're on the path God has for us so that we end up in the right place. The way to do that is to walk closely with God, live in obedience to His ways, and be led by His Spirit so that we are moving in His will. However, just as some men won't ask for directions when they are driving, there are some men who won't ask for direction from God when they are traveling the highway of their life, either.

It's not that this never happens to a woman, but most women seem to quickly recognize when they have taken a wrong turn.

Some men don't realize they are on the wrong road until they have fallen off of a cliff. But the good news about that is a wife's prayers for her husband can keep him headed in the right direction, or at least help him recognize his lack of a spiritual GPS in time to avoid total disaster.

God never pushes against a strong will, nor does He force a stubborn person to submit. If your husband has either of those characteristics, pray he will not be guided by his ego. Pray he won't have such faith in his own judgment that he refuses to seek the wisdom and will of God. If your husband has already chosen a wrong path and you or he are paying for it in some way right now, ask God to redeem the situation. Even when you cannot see a way out, *He* can. Ask God to do whatever it takes to get your husband headed in the right direction. If he is on a good path right now, keep praying that he continues to stay on it.

My Prayer to God

Lord, I pray You would keep my husband on the path You have for Him. Take away all deception and open his eyes to see Your truth. Fill him with Your Spirit so that he will move in wisdom. Where there is stubbornness or rebellion in him, break down those walls of resistance to Your ways. Don't let him be so self-reliant that he refuses to depend on You. Surround him with wise men so that he will make wise choices (Proverbs 13:20). I pray he will see that You, Lord, are the way, and he must walk close to You.

Where he has already gotten on the wrong path and we are experiencing the consequences of that, I pray You would enable him to be on the right path—the path You have for him—and that You would help him stay on it. Keep him on the road that leads to life. Convict his heart strongly and quickly whenever he strays from Your will. Give him a thoroughly repentant heart for all that has been wasted whenever he has walked willfully and not prayerfully. Help me to maintain a right heart before You and not fall into resentment because of consequences I am experiencing due to mistakes he has made. Lead him, Holy Spirit, for only then will *all* his steps be headed in the right direction (Galatians 5:25). I know we cannot walk the narrow path You have for us without Your guidance.

In Jesus' name I pray.

72

When We Should Be Anxious for Nothing

Be anxious for nothing, but in everything
by prayer and supplication,
with thanksgiving, let your requests
be made known to God*;*
and the peace of God*, which surpasses*
all understanding,
will guard your hearts and minds
through Christ Jesus*.*

PHILIPPIANS 4:6-7

ANXIETY IS SUCH a waste of time and energy for a believer. It is not only exhausting and depleting, it doesn't get us anywhere. Of course, if we didn't know the Lord and did not have His Holy Spirit living in us, we would certainly have reason to be anxious. For then our life would be on the line every day and one failure could destroy it. But not so with those of us who walk with God. We already recognize that *without Him* we can do nothing lasting and good. And we also know that when tough times happen, we can pray and God will give us a peace that cannot be found any other way.

When difficult things happen in your life, go immediately to God and give your burden to Him. Offer up praise and worship, no matter how low you feel. Thank Him that He is the God of the universe for whom nothing is impossible. Pray specifically about the situation you are in, tell Him what you want Him to do, explain to Him how you feel, and don't stop until you have that peace that is beyond comprehension. This means it won't make sense that you have such peace in the situation you're in except that it has come from God.

The peace God gives you puts a shield around your heart and mind. It takes control away from your fear and doubt. It evaporates anxiety. There is a distinct connection between prayer and the peace of God. So at the first sign of anxiety, go where you know peace can be found. Why give anxiety a moment of your time when you can pray about what is making you anxious? Pray for yourself and your husband that anxiety has no place in either of your hearts. Pray you will not waste your time and energy on something so unnecessary.

My Prayer to God

LORD, I pray You would help my husband and me to reject anxiety at the first sign of it. No matter what is happening, help us to turn to You in prayer. Teach us how to truly cast our fears, cares, and burdens on You. Enable us to pray in power about the things that are heavy on our hearts, always praising and thanking You that You hear our prayers and answer in Your way and Your time.

I specifically lift up to You the concerns that are heaviest on our hearts right now. Thank You that as we give these cares to You, You will give us Your peace that is beyond what we could ever know on our own. I pray Your peace will be so deep in our hearts that it will protect our minds from being eaten up with fearful thoughts and our strength from being depleted by exhausting worry. Remind us to share our concerns with You right away and not waste valuable time and energy entertaining anxiety. Help us to be anxious for nothing. Thank You for Your amazing peace that triumphs over all our fears.

In Jesus' name I pray.

73

When I Think of Divorce as an Option

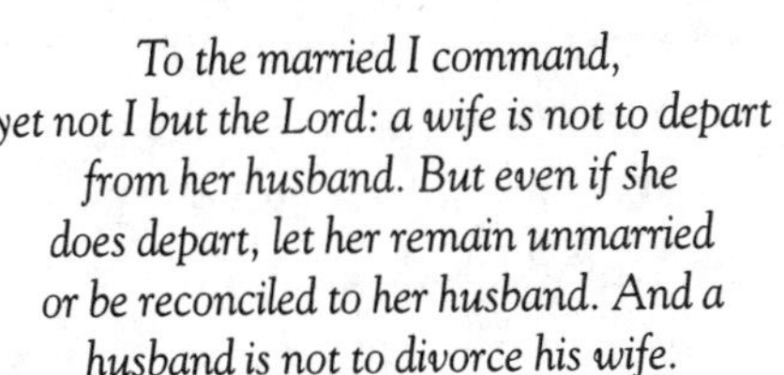

To the married I command,
yet not I but the Lord: a wife is not to depart
from her husband. But even if she
does depart, let her remain unmarried
or be reconciled to her husband. And a
husband is not to divorce his wife.

1 Corinthians 7:10-11

GOD IS CLEAR ABOUT His attitude regarding divorce. He hates it. "The Lord God of Israel says that He hates divorce" (Malachi 2:16). "Hate" is a strong word. In fact, we don't like the idea that the almighty God of the universe might hate anything we do. But when a marriage becomes like hell on earth, and the pain of it is more than we can bear, and it seems like there is no way of reconciliation available to us, our thoughts can turn to the "D" word as a way out.

The best way to combat thoughts of divorce is to bring them to the Lord in confession and prayer *immediately* when they come to mind and not allow them to fester and grow into something big. One of the reasons we don't do that is because we are either already totally convinced there is no other way, or we are embarrassed before God to even confess to Him that we have those thoughts. It also could be that we long so to be free of the pain the marriage is causing that we want out no matter what. But God wants us to expose that dark thinking to His light so He can burn it out of us and change the situation.

If you ever begin thinking of divorce as an option, don't give that thought a chance to grow. The enemy of your soul and your marriage will take the thought as a seed and plant it in your heart, and feed it with lies until it grows into something bigger than you ever thought it could. Ask God to help you crush that seed while it is still small. He is more than pleased to enable you to stand strong against something He so adamantly hates.

My Prayer to God

LORD, I confess to You as sin any time I have ever allowed even one thought of divorce to stay in my mind as a viable solution to our problems. I know divorce is not Your will and You hate a broken covenant. I ask that You would pour out Your Spirit on my husband and me, and teach us to love and respect each other enough to communicate well and work things out between us. Change each of us in every way we need to be changed so that we can be better together.

Where it feels that something has been mortally wounded

between us, I pray You would breathe new life into our hearts and minds. Take away all hardness and work a miracle of forgiveness in each of us. Help us to apologize and ask forgiveness every time it is warranted. Teach us to want to serve and please You more than we want to serve and please ourselves. I pray that there will be no divorce in our future. Where there has been a divorce in either of our pasts, I pray You would forgive us and teach us how to keep it from ever happening again. Keep us both from falling into the trap of thinking that divorce is the only way out of pain.

In Jesus' name I pray.

74

When He Leaves Home for an Extended Time

I will go in the strength of the Lord God;
I will make mention of Your
righteousness, of Yours only.

PSALM 71:16

I KNOW A YOUNG WOMAN whose husband is in the military, serving in Iraq for his second deployment of fourteen months. This is a great sacrifice for a newly married couple with a toddler and a baby on the way. She handles it well, even though it must be unbearably hard for them, because they both know the Lord and believe in the power of staying close by praying for each other.

There are many reasons a man might have to be away from his wife and family for an extended period of time—work being probably the most common one. If you have to be separated from your husband by a great distance or large blocks of time, prayer is what can keep you closely connected. If it is a separation that you both agree is the right thing, then the results will be good. If one of you doesn't think the separation is right, this can present a problem. However, if both of you agree to pray for each other during the time you are apart, good things will come of it.

If you are praying for each other every day, then after the separation is over it will almost be as though it never happened because you are able to pick up right where you left off. Praying for him is something *you* must do, even if your husband is not doing it along with you. No matter how far away your husband is, or how long he is gone, pray that he goes and comes back safely.

My Prayer to God

LORD, I pray any time my husband and I have to be separated by a great distance or for a long time that You will keep him protected. Bring him home safe and uninjured. Help him to do well in all that he must do, and enable him to do what is right. Give him wisdom to work well with the people around him, but keep him from all temptation. Draw him closer to You during this time, and don't allow him to drift away. Even though we are separated by time and space, I pray You would draw us closer together than we even were before he left.

Help me to grow in You while he is gone, so that when he returns I am a better person. Help me to make our home a welcome place for him to return to. When he comes home, I pray he will be able to readjust quickly. Help us to immediately be compatible, comfortable, and in harmony with each other. If there are any tensions, unresolved conflicts, or hard feelings that have not been resolved before he leaves, I pray You will resolve them in us by the power of Your Holy Spirit, even as I am praying for him every day.

Help us to remember the best in each other and not the worst, and think about the good times and not the bad. Protect our marriage so that we continue growing together and not apart. Protect his going out and coming in so that he returns "in the strength of the Lord," and enable him to not forget for a moment about You and Your ways.

In Jesus' name I pray.

75

When We Must Become One

I will give them one heart,
and I will put a new spirit within them,
and take the stony heart out of their flesh,
and give them a heart of flesh, that
they may walk in My statutes and
keep My judgments and do them;
and they shall be My people,
and I will be their God.

EZEKIEL 11:19-20

GOD'S WORD SAYS He made a husband and wife to be one (Genesis 2:24). That's the way He sees you and your husband. But it's important that you both see yourselves that way too. As a couple, you must choose to move in the same direction of oneness. The other alternative is to *not* make any such choice and then watch yourselves automatically move in separate directions. That's because in the busyness of your lives, self-focus will be the natural outcome. But if you deliberately make the choice to become one, and pray for that, it will cause you and your husband to grow deeper in love and respect.

How often do we see marriages progress in the exact opposite direction, where what grows between a husband and wife is contempt and dislike? Far too often. It's heartbreaking to watch that happening when God wants to prevent it or reverse it. If you and your husband ever allow yourselves to become critical of each other, constantly judging all that you dislike about each other, or refusing to put the other person before yourself, ask God on behalf of your husband to give you both a new spirit and a united heart. Ask Him to take away any hardness of heart that has developed and to soften your hearts toward each other. Pray that He will help you grow together in love, respect, communication, esteem, and friendship.

It is crucial to pray that God will work complete forgiveness in your hearts toward each other so that all resentment, judgment, and contempt are gone and His Spirit can unify you. Even if none of this has ever happened to you and your husband, pray that it never will. Pray that every day you will continue to become more and more one—just as God sees you now.

My Prayer to God

LORD, I know You have made my husband and me to be one, but there are times when our selfish pursuits have gotten in the way of that. Where we have pursued our own interests and not Yours, I confess that to You as sin. Forgive us and keep us from working against Your will in that regard. Give us one heart and a new spirit so that we can walk together on the path You have for us.

I pray it is Your Spirit poured out in us that rules our lives. Only You, Lord, have the power to transform us and take away our selfishness, critical spirit, contempt, disrespect, or separateness. Pour Your love into our hearts, minds, and souls so that it rules like the powerful life-changing force it is. Break the back of any hard-heartedness in either of us. Give us softened hearts that can be molded by Your hand to become what You want them to be. Help us to grow together and not apart. While You already see us as one, I pray You would enable us to walk in the oneness of soul, spirit, and purpose You have called us to.

In Jesus' name I pray.

76

When I Need Emotional Restoration

He heals the brokenhearted and
binds up their wounds.

Psalm 147:3

TOO OFTEN WE WOMEN accept a lie from the enemy as truth in our lives. The enemy tells us we can never get free of negative emotions such as sadness, loneliness, anxiety, fear, depression, feelings of failure, hopelessness, anger, or whatever else. But that is a major deception. And deception will happen to anyone who is not deliberately seeking the Spirit of truth. We need to frequently ask God to help us remain undeceived so we can be free of negative emotions. Negative emotions are the opposite of what God has for us.

King David said of the Lord, "He restores my soul" (Psalm 23:3). In fact, the entire Twenty-third Psalm is healing to your soul and you should read it often. Being in God's presence also brings emotional healing because He brings wholeness to every part of your life. That's why praise and worship, along with the Word of God, is your greatest weapon against negative emotions. When you feel the constraints of negative emotions trying to control you, lift up praise to God and thank Him that He restores health to your soul and heals you of your wounds (Jeremiah 30:17).

Whatever you have struggled with in your emotions, name it before the Lord and ask Him to heal and renew you. Ask God to set you free from all doubt in His ability and desire to heal your soul completely. Don't settle for anything less than the emotional wholeness God has for you. He wants to restore your soul and lead you in paths of righteousness. He wants you to know that His "goodness and mercy" will follow you all the days of your life (Psalm 23:6).

My Prayer to God

LORD, I thank You that You are the healer of my soul. Thank You that in Your presence I can find freedom from all negative emotions. I lift to You the specific negative emotions I am dealing with lately and ask that You would deliver me from them. Where there are wounds of my soul needing to be healed that I am not seeing, reveal them to me so that I can bring them to You in prayer. I don't want to continue another day entangled in any yoke of oppression from which You want me liberated.

I lift up praise to You and thank You that in Your presence I can find freedom from everything that keeps me from becoming all You created me to be. Open my eyes so I can see any negative emotions in my life as unacceptable. Work in me Your perfect rejuvenation, cleansing, and restoration of my soul. Take away all sadness, depression, anxiety, fear, hopelessness, self-focus, emotional pain, and whatever else I am living with that is not Your will for my life.

I know that any negative emotions I have will greatly affect my husband and my marriage. I don't want anything like that affecting my life, especially when You have a way for me to be free. Keep me from being deceived by the lies of the enemy, who seeks to make me think that this is the way I have to be. Renew me in my mind and soul. Set me free from all negative emotions so I can live in the wholeness You have for me.

In Jesus' name I pray.

77

When He Is Injured

This is my comfort in my affliction,
for Your word has given me life.

Psalm 119:50

MEN DO NOT LIKE to be incapacitated. Women don't like it either, but most tend to be less miserable about it with regard to everyone around them. Pain can help us straighten out a bad attitude, or it can make a bad attitude even worse, depending on how we react to it. No one likes to be injured or in pain, but even in our misery we still can choose to glorify God. The way to do this is by frequently praising God that He is our healer and deliverer, which opens up the channel by which He pours forth healing and deliverance in our life. Your prayers and praise can help your husband not only find the healing and deliverance he needs, but also maintain a right attitude in the process.

The Bible says to "pray for one another, that you may be healed" (James 5:16). It goes on to say that the "effective fervent prayer of a righteous man avails much." Your fervent prayers for your husband have great power and effectiveness. Make it a habit to pray for protection from injury *before* anything happens. When you do that and an injury or accident still happens, the results can be miraculously minor compared to what they could have been.

If an injury has already happened, pray not only for the healing touch of God upon his body and mind, but also pray that he will be able to discern whether this is caused by an attack of the enemy. Understanding this can encourage him to be mad at the devil and not at God. If it is caused by something he has foolishly done, pray for revelation and wisdom about that. Or if it happened through no fault of his own, pray that he not be bitter. No matter what happens, thank God that He is your healer and He can restore brokenness in body as well as in soul and spirit.

My Prayer to God

Lord, I pray You would protect my husband from any accidents or injuries. Keep him safe wherever he goes. Where he has already been injured, I pray You would heal him. Take away his pain and discomfort. Lead him to the right doctors, and help them to make the correct diagnosis and prescribe the proper treatment. Give wisdom to all the doctors and therapists he sees so that they can help him to recover speedily.

Teach him whatever he must know in order to prevent this from happening in the future. Show him what he needs to *stop doing* in order to avoid further injury. Reveal whatever he should *start doing* that would strengthen him to avoid future injuries. Show me how I can help him. Give me fresh insight and Holy Spirit–led knowledge as to what to do for him.

I pray that his attitude will be right before You so that he will not be angry at his condition, or at You, or at me, or at anyone else. Help him to see that an attitude of praise and worship toward You at all times is far more healing than a negative or bitter attitude, which only further affects his body in a bad way. May he be comforted by Your presence and find restoration in You.

In Jesus' name I pray.

78

When We Need God's Word to Come Alive in Us

The word of God is living and powerful,
and sharper than any two-edged sword,
piercing even to the division of
soul and spirit, and of joints and marrow,
and is a discerner of the thoughts and intents of the heart.

HEBREWS 4:12

EVERY TIME WE READ the Bible we see new things we didn't see before. Even a Scripture we have read a hundred times can take us to a new understanding and revelation of God on the one-hundred-first time we read it. That is one of the reasons the Word of God is so profound. It is living. It is Holy Spirit breathed. And every time we read it, it is etched deeper in our mind and becomes more pronounced and alive in our heart. The more we read, the more we believe. A life without the Word of God in our mind and heart is empty and powerless.

Both you and your husband need all the life and power God has for you, especially with regard to your marriage. That's why you must pray to have God's Word etched in your heart in such a way that it increases your faith in Him and His truth. Pray that both of you will be drawn to read God's Word and retain it, and to understand it in ever-deepening ways. Pray it will come alive in your hearts.

If your husband doesn't know the Lord, speak God's Word over him in prayer, and pray that it will penetrate his heart in such a way that his eyes will be open to see the truth. If he knows the Lord but is resistant to reading the Bible, pray for him to feel his emptiness without it. Pray that he will be drawn to it and find the fullness of the Lord in it. Pray that God's Word will be implanted in his heart and grow into a big faith that is living and powerful.

My Prayer to God

LORD, I thank You that Your Word is living and powerful. I pray my husband and I will deepen our desire for more of Your Word to be resident in our hearts and minds. Open our eyes to see Your truth. Help us to retain it so that it becomes part of our memory and our thoughts. Imprint it in our hearts so that it always reminds us of how we should live. Where either of us is resistant to reading Your Word, take away our rebelliousness. Teach us to long for more of Your living truth and more of You in our lives. Increase our faith every time we read or speak Your Word, as You have promised to do.

I pray we will learn to believe Your Word so firmly that we cannot be shaken by influences around us that voice thoughts contrary to what is Your truth. Your Word is living and powerful enough to expose the thoughts and plans of our hearts, so every time we read it, reveal any wrong thinking in us. When my husband will not read it himself, I pray he will be open to my reading it to him or will allow me to speak it over him in prayer. Help us to love You with all of our heart, soul, mind, and strength (Mark 12:30). And by doing so, I pray You will impart to us greater understanding of Your Word than we have ever had before.

In Jesus' name I pray.

79

When I Want to Be Transformed

We all, with unveiled face, beholding
as in a mirror the glory of the Lord,
are being transformed into the same image
from glory to glory,
just as by the Spirit of the Lord.

2 CORINTHIANS 3:18

WE ALL NEED to be changed. There is no doubt about that. This is because we all need to become more like the Lord. But the only way we can become more like Him is to spend time with Him and look to Him for everything. We spend time with Him when we pray, when we worship and praise Him, when we look into His Word in order to know Him better, and when we hear Him speaking to our hearts about Himself. The more we look to Him, the more we begin to reflect His character, and the more we are transformed into His image. We always reflect what we behold. As we continue to behold Him, we go from glory to glory by the power of the Holy Spirit.

You already recognize when you need transformation in your life, but there are times when you are more acutely aware of it than others. If you are depleted, exhausted, sick, messed up in your mind or emotions, or plagued with faulty thinking, or if something bad happens and you don't react well, you know you need a fresh infusion of the restorative power of the Holy Spirit. It is God's will that you find His transformation, but He wants you to pray for it.

Ask God often for the transformation He has for you. Ask Him to help you spend more time with Him so you can get to know Him better. Pray that He will reveal Himself more and more to you as you follow Him. When you desire to be renewed and changed into all God made you to be, seek Him for it and He will bless you with it. Ask Him to enable you to go from glory to glory by beholding *His* glory and being transformed into His image.

My Prayer to God

Lord, I am very aware of my own limitations. I know there are times when I can be less than I want to be in patience, compassion, kindness, and love. But I also know You can change me and transform me into Your likeness. I need You to do that now. I know that in You is found perfect patience, compassion, kindness, and unconditional love. I need those attributes every day, but never more than in my marriage and my relationship with my husband. Help me to be more like You so that I can be the wife You want me to be for him. I know that I don't have it in me to reflect Your wonderful characteristics on my own, so I look to You for help.

As I look to You every day, I ask that Your reflection will be revealed increasingly in me. Change me according to Your will. Continue to renew my mind and heart so that I can find the transformation You have for my soul and my life. Instill such peace in me that I am never without it, no matter what is happening in our circumstances. Help me to communicate your goodness to my husband in ways that inspire it in him. Bestow upon me *Your* patience, compassion, kindness, and love in increasing measure until others can clearly see those attributes in me. Enable me to behold Your presence as I worship You so I can go from glory to glory, until Your goodness, love, and beauty are revealed in my heart.

In Jesus' name I pray.

80

When He Must Make Peace with His Father

Honor your father and your mother,
as the Lord your God has commanded you,
that your days may be long, and that it
may be well with you in the land
which the Lord your God is giving you.

DEUTERONOMY 5:16

ONE OF THE MOST important things your husband can do in order to receive all God has for him is to make peace with his father. Whether he had a great father, or an absent one, or a cruel father who is no longer living, he still has to come to a place of forgiveness and release so he can honor him in his heart.

When Noah was sleeping and became uncovered, one of his sons, Ham, went into his tent and saw his nakedness. Instead of covering his father, he went to his brothers and told them what he had seen. His brothers, Shem and Japheth, took a garment and walked backward into their father's tent and covered him. Because of their respect for their father, they were blessed. Because of Ham's disrespect, he was cursed. These blessings and curses followed the people and nations that descended accordingly from Noah's three sons from then on (Genesis 9:18-27).

This curse is serious. God promises that by honoring your father and mother you will have a long and good life. But He declares that *not* honoring them means your life will not go well and it will be cut short. If the image in your husband's mind of his father is a negative one because of things his father has done or not done, pray for your husband to be healed of those memories. That doesn't mean he will completely forget what happened. It means the memories will no longer have the power to continue making him suffer.

The Bible also says that one who disrespects his father or mother is deserving of death (Matthew 15:4). How much death do people experience in their lives by not observing this law? It's worth praying about, because this is an issue that is many layers thick for most men. The peace—or lack thereof—in your husband's heart regarding his relationship with his father will not only greatly affect *him*, but it will affect *you* as well.

My Prayer to God

LORD, I pray You will take away any negative memories my husband has of his father. I know You do not want him to disrespect his father in any way, but You *do* want him to enjoy all the blessings You have for him. Heal any hurt, bitterness, anger, sadness, apathy, or painful memory that is in his heart toward his father. Help him to do what is necessary to completely clear the slate.

Where my husband has felt his father was too strong or too weak, give him insight as to why he was the way he was. Where he might feel there was a lack of love coming from his father, help him to know You as his heavenly Father who loves him unconditionally. Where he may have felt abandoned in some way by his father, help him to see that You will never leave or forsake him. Even if he had a great father, I pray he will forgive any bad memories of past incidents. Whether his father is living or deceased, I pray there will be reconciliation between them, at least from my husband's standpoint. Heal that relationship—or lack of—as only You can do.

In Jesus' name I pray.

81

When We Need to Resist All Sexual Pollution

Turn away my eyes from
looking at worthless things,
and revive me in Your way.

PSALM 119:37

NOT ONLY DO WE not want sexual immorality to creep into our marriage, we don't want sexual pollution in our minds, either. Sexual pollution is everywhere. We even see it in such harmless places as news magazines, billboards, films, commercials, television, and on the Internet. Just because we have never viewed pornography doesn't mean our mind isn't already polluted. This is a big issue for too many marriages, so don't think because *you* are not enticed by it that your husband can never be influenced in that way.

The enemy's plan for your marriage and your soul is to distract you from God's best with images that can pollute your sexual relationship. God wants sex in your marriage to reaffirm your oneness. The enemy wants to destroy that oneness. Pornography is an enormous issue today because of easy access to it on the Internet. It has often been justified by those who view it saying, "It's not hurting anyone." But it is not only hurting the person who views it, it also hurts that person's relationship with their spouse. When a man is found to be viewing pornography, the pain it causes his wife is beyond description.

All sexual immorality is destructive, even if it is "only" in the mind. Just as physical immorality destroys the body, mental immorality destroys the mind, and affairs of the heart destroy the soul. The damage is never worth whatever momentary pleasure the person thinks they are deriving from it. Even if your husband wouldn't dream of doing anything like that, pray for him anyway. Pray that he will be successful in resisting the sexual pollution that pervades our society. Pray that you both can resist this plan of the enemy to destroy your marriage.

My Prayer to God

LORD, I pray You will strengthen my husband and me by the power of Your Holy Spirit, and help us to stand strong against any enticing or lustful spirit that would cause either of us to allow ourselves to be polluted in our minds with illicit sexual images. Smash down any temptation we ever face that would allow any kind of sexual pollution to infect our lives. Enable us to immediately recognize the threat and resist it by fleeing from it. I know that a thought can overtake our mind and grow into action even as we are thinking we are well able to handle it. I pray that pornography never enters our experience or our home at any time. Smash down that evil so it has no place in our lives whatsoever.

Keep us from violating Your laws of sexual purity in any way. Help each of us to take our mind captive so that we don't allow sexual pollution to invade it. Where there has already been a violation of Your laws with regard to this, in either my husband or me, I pray You would bring it to light so that we can come with repentant hearts to be cleansed of all sin and delivered from any hold it has on us. If nothing like this has happened to either of us, work complete purity in our hearts so that we stay protected from all sexual pollution in body, mind, and soul.

In Jesus' name I pray.

82

When I Should Take Better Care of My Body

Do you not know that your body is the temple of the Holy Spirit who is in you, whom you have from God, and you are not your own? For you were bought at a price; therefore glorify God in your body and in your spirit, which are God's.

1 Corinthians 6:19-20

MOST WOMEN ARE busy taking care of their family, or working to help support them, or both. The probability is good that you are stretched to the limit with responsibilities, caretaking, and life's other activities. Something has to give, and it may be that what is sacrificed in your life is time spent caring for your own body. Too often a woman feels guilty if she takes time to do things for herself, as if she is being selfish. She often feels that only what she does for *others* is important. But this is not true.

It's part of her service to the Lord that a woman not neglect herself physically, mentally, or spiritually.

It is not good for you, your family, or your marriage to neglect taking time to care for *you*. You must recognize that your body is the temple of the Holy Spirit and not your own. Jesus paid a high price for you, and He wants you to glorify Him by taking good care of yourself. That means spending time before the Lord every day in prayer and worship, in order to grow closer to God and be able to rest your mind from concerns. That means you need to eat foods that build up, strengthen, and increase your vitality and health, not foods that weaken, sicken, or destroy. It means exercising your body consistently in some way that rejuvenates, renews, and strengthens you. All these things affect your inner self as well as your physical health.

Ask God to show you what to do. Put the care of your body in His hands. Don't underestimate how attractive physical health, strength, and vitality are to your husband. It is not selfish to want that and to make the effort to find it.

My Prayer to God

LORD, I pray You would show me how to properly care for my body so that I can enjoy good health, renewed strength, and more energy. By doing so, help me to be the kind of pleasant and attractive person I want to be and that my husband and children enjoy being around. Help me to take the time to eat the right foods that give me life and health. Help me to be disciplined enough to exercise properly and consistently so that I can be strong and energetic. Most of all, help me to spend private time with You every day so I can find the peace and refreshment that only You can give me. Enable me to get sound, rejuvenating rest at night so that I can maintain good health and greater mental clarity throughout the day.

Show me all I need to do to properly care for my body as the temple of Your Spirit. Help me to not feel guilty about taking time and making the effort to do something for myself that is ultimately beneficial to my husband and my family. Enable me to be rid of all exhaustion and weakness so I can concentrate. In doing all these things, help me to glorify You in my body and spirit, which are Yours.

In Jesus' name I pray.

83

When He Needs to Have a Cheerful Heart

A merry heart does good, like medicine,
but a broken spirit dries the bones.

PROVERBS 17:22

WE CAN ALL WORK OURSELVES into attitudes that are negative. We may become so afraid of bad news that we anticipate it with negative thoughts and words. Our spirit can be so broken that negativity becomes an automatic response to everything without us even realizing it. Habits of the heart like this are hard to break, but by the power of God they can be changed in an instant.

If your husband has those kinds of negative thoughts, they will not only bring *him* down, but they will bring *you* down as well. It's hard to be around someone who is always negative. It may be that *you* are the one who has a chronically heavy heart and it is bringing *him* down. Or possibly you have a heavy heart in reaction to *his*. Whatever the situation, pray that God will change all that. Pray for your husband to be healed of a broken spirit and filled with the Spirit of God so that the joy of the Lord can rise in him. Pray for him to experience the presence of God so that he becomes convinced of who God is and all He has done for him. Pray that he be reminded every day that because of God he is never without hope.

Ask God to take away a heavy heart from your husband and keep him from getting sick because of it. We all need the medicine that comes from a heart lifted up in cheer and joyful anticipation of what God is going to do next in our lives. Ask God to give your husband the medicine of a merry heart as a gift for *both* of you.

My Prayer to God

Lord, I pray for my husband to have a cheerful heart that is like a medicine for him. Fill him with Your joy until it overflows and evaporates all heaviness. Cause joy to rise up from within him like an endless well connected to the flow of Your Spirit. Fill him afresh with Your Holy Spirit each day, and don't let anything keep good cheer and lightheartedness from swelling up in him. I pray the same for me. Fill me with Your good cheer as well, so that it sweeps away any dark clouds of heaviness. Where I have felt sad in reaction to my husband's heavy heart, I pray You would strengthen me to rise above that.

Give my husband and me Your joy so that it will be healing for each of us and for our marriage. Only You can do that. And only our love of You can stir it up within us.

Show each of us whenever we think negative thoughts or have anticipation in our heart that expects something bad to happen. Break any habits of my husband's heart that are negative, so that his response to every situation is a positive expectation of the good things You are doing in his life and in our lives together.

In Jesus' name I pray.

84

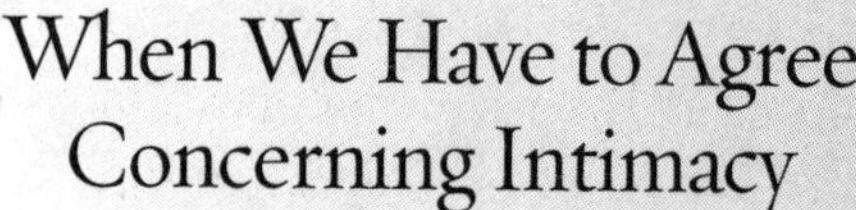

When We Have to Agree Concerning Intimacy

Do not deprive one another except
with consent for a time,
that you may give yourselves to fasting
and prayer; and come together again
so that Satan does not tempt you because
of your lack of self-control.

1 CORINTHIANS 7:5

A HUSBAND AND WIFE'S sexual relationship is a vital part of any marriage, and yet it is often neglected, not talked about, not agreed upon with regard to specifics, and too often not prayed about. We must remember that God created marital intimacy and designed it, and He said it was good. It is up to us to keep it that way. As a couple, you and your husband must be in agreement about the details. If it is not a mutual agreement, one or the other will be frustrated or dissatisfied. And it must be a priority for both of you so that proper effort is put into seeing that this area of the marriage is not put low on a list of "things to do." And this can easily happen in the busyness, stress, and exhaustion of our days and weeks.

Pray that you and your husband will keep the physical and emotional fires alive in your marriage. Ask God to help you both communicate your needs to each other. This is not something to leave to chance, or to ignore and see what happens. Many marriages have been destroyed over this issue.

If a husband or wife is being neglected in this area, then there is no agreement. Even though sexual needs may change as the years go by, there should be communication about that too. Deprivation is a problem, and one person should not have to suffer that. Intimacy is an important part of life. Prayer and communication are the answers to working this out to the satisfaction of both of you. And it is far easier to pray in advance than it is to pray after there is a problem.

My Prayer to God

LORD, I pray You would bless our sexual relationship so that it will be fulfilling for each of us. Help us to have a workable understanding about it so that we always agree on the frequency and manner of how it progresses. Enable us to have open communication so that we understand each other's needs. Teach us to be sensitive to each other so that our needs are met in a good and reasonable way. Help us both make this part of our relationship a priority so that we make time and an effort for it. Keep us from ever pushing it to the back of our to-do list, ignoring the needs of our spouse.

Help us to make this important part of our lives satisfying to each other.

Where our desires are in opposition, I pray You would help us to be understanding and able to come to an agreement. If I have closed off in this area, help me to open up to him again the way I should. Where he has closed off, help him to warm to me again so that our physical expression of love is natural and easy, the way You made it to be. Keep us from withholding ourselves from each other for any reason. I know from Your Word that this is against what You want for us. Take away all negativity in our hearts with regard to giving ourselves to each other, and free us to be open and desiring of each other in every way.

In Jesus' name I pray.

85

When I Must Forgive All Other People

Whenever you stand praying,
if you have anything against anyone,
forgive him, that your Father in heaven
may also forgive you your trespasses.

MARK 11:25

WHILE FORGIVING YOUR HUSBAND is crucial in order for your marriage to succeed, it is also extremely important for you to forgive all others as well. That's because *any* unforgiveness in your heart will form a roadblock to the pathway of answered prayer you so desire. Jesus said if you start to pray and have *anything* against another person, you must forgive that person so God can forgive you.

When we have unconfessed sin, God will not listen to our prayers. "If I regard iniquity in my heart, the Lord will not hear" (Psalm 66:18). That's because unforgiveness is one of the greatest sins, and God will not tolerate it in us. Jesus gave His life for us so that we can be totally forgiven of our past sins and not have to bear the consequences of them. But the sins we commit now *do* have consequences, and until we confess and repent of them, He will hold off on listening to our prayers. It's not that He *can't* hear them; it's that He *won't* hear them until we clear away whatever is putting up a barrier from *our* side. We cannot afford to have God not listening to our prayers. We need His answers. In order for God to hear your prayers for your marriage, you *must* forgive *everyone* of *anything* you have against them.

Not only is unforgiveness unacceptable to God, it is usually unattractive to other people as well. They see it in you, even if they don't recognize what it is. Your husband sees it in you too. You may not have any unforgiveness toward him, but he will notice the unforgiveness you have toward others even if he doesn't know that's what he is observing. Unforgiveness is way too heavy a burden to carry. Give it to the Lord and let Him have it all.

My Prayer to God

Lord, I pray You would show me every person in my life whom I need to forgive. Reveal to me anyone I *believe* I have already forgiven but am still retaining some unforgiveness toward in my heart. I know layers of unforgiveness can be hidden under our good intentions, and I don't want that to exist in my life. I don't want any unconfessed sin to be a hindrance to Your hearing and answering my prayers. I desire to always be forgiving of others just as You have forgiven me (Colossians 3:13).

I know I cannot move forward into all You have for me

until I forget "those things which are behind" (Philippians 3:13). But I need Your help to do so. Show me when avoiding, criticizing, dismissing, or withdrawing are signs of hanging on to an unresolved past offense. I want to confess anything I need to so that I can move on in my life and experience the answers to my prayers. Because I desire Your forgiveness of *my* sins and errors, I choose this day to forgive all others in my life. Show me also if there is anyone who has something against me, someone from whom I need to seek forgiveness. Give me the words to say to resolve that. More than anything else, I want to live Your way, and I know that Your way is always the path of forgiveness.

In Jesus' name I pray.

86

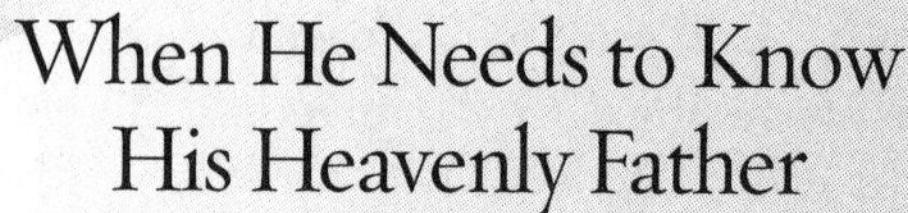

When He Needs to Know His Heavenly Father

When my father and my mother forsake me,
then the Lord will take care of me.

Psalm 27:10

EVERY YOUNG BOY NEEDS a father to help him become a man. Most boys who never had a father—or at least not one they remember in their lives, or who lost their father at an early age for one reason or another, or who did not have a strong and loving father figure—suffer for it later on. We see examples of this all the time. Even if a boy did have a father in his home, but that father was missing-in-action because of selfishness, preoccupation, apathy, workaholism, alcohol, drugs, gambling, or whatever else, there will be a major hole in this grown-up young man's heart that can only be filled by knowing his heavenly Father intimately.

In whatever way your husband may have lacked a good relationship with his father, or if he has hurtful memories of his father, or if his father was not nurturing and loving, pray that your husband comes to know his Father God's love in a way that can fill any empty place in him and heal those wounds. Pray he will come to trust that his heavenly Father will never abandon, ignore, or reject him, but instead will always have time for him and will continually pour everything He has into him.

Your husband needs to know that his heavenly Father has an inheritance for him that is far beyond anything his earthly father could ever give him. It is a life of eternal security and the fulfillment of every need in this life. Your prayers for your husband about this can change his life forever. And it will definitely change your marriage for the better too.

My Prayer to God

LORD, I thank You that You are a Father to us (2 Corinthians 6:18). I pray that my husband will know You intimately as his heavenly Father. Whatever was lacking in his relationship with his earthly father, I pray You will redeem and supply. Heal any wounds he has suffered because of it. As his heavenly Father, teach him all he needs to know in order to become a man that he wasn't taught by his earthly father. Only You can heal any damage that happened in the past and bring him to complete wholeness in You. Help him to forgive his earthly father for anything that was lacking in his life so that he will not put on You whatever was missing in his dad.

I pray the same for myself. Where my earthly dad did not model for me what a father should have, and I have judged my husband in light of it—where my father did not come through for me, and now I fear my husband won't come through for me, either—I confess that before You. Forgive me and free me to know You as my heavenly Father in a depth I have not known before. Wherever my husband has projected onto You the weaknesses or imperfection of his earthly father, I pray You will set him free from that. Help him to see You fully, in all Your strength and perfection, as his heavenly Father who loves him and who will never forsake him.

In Jesus' name I pray.

87

When We Must Trust God to Work Everything Out for Good

We know that all things work together
for good to those who love God,
to those who are the called
according to His purpose.

ROMANS 8:28

THERE ARE TIMES IN OUR LIVES and in our marriages when something happens and we don't see how we can ever rise above it, or get through it, or get over it. At these times we must cling to God and take Him at His Word. He says that all things work out for good to those who love Him and are submitted to His purpose in their lives. But the verses before that one are talking about prayer. It seems, then, that things work out for good when we are praying. And that makes sense, doesn't it? God works powerfully in our lives when we pray.

Whenever you are facing something insurmountable in your life—such as a financial disaster, the loss of a family member, problems with a child, serious illness, or any of the many dreadful things that can happen—invite God to do something in your situation that your mind can't even conceive of or never thought possible. Keep praying, no matter how hopeless it seems, and don't stop thanking God that He works out everything in your lives for good when you love and trust Him for your future.

If you don't have any kind of serious problem right now, praise God for that. Thank Him that He is the God of the impossible, and if you *were* to have anything seemingly insurmountable happen to you in the future, you trust that He will work everything out for good. In the meantime, continue staying close to Him in prayer, and pray for your husband to do the same.

My Prayer to God

Lord, I thank You that because I love and serve You and pray about all things—and because I desire Your will to be done in my husband's and my life together—that You will work all things out for good. The situation in our lives that seems insurmountable to us today is not too hard for You. Even though we cannot see a way out of that problem, I know *You* can. While we alone don't have what it takes to rise above the difficulty, I know You have everything needed to lift us above it or carry us through it. Even when a situation may be a tragedy to us, You can still bring good out of it. Even though we cannot imagine what good can possibly come from it, we can trust Your miracle-working power to transform the situation.

I pray You will bring restoration where there has been

loss. Give us peace when, without You, we would have none. Teach us to pray first, instead of being overtaken by discouragement or fear. Enable us to learn from every problem so that we can be a help to others in the same situation. Most of all, give us great faith to firmly trust You and Your Word in the midst of the storm, knowing You are bringing a bright tomorrow, even as we pray.

In Jesus' name I pray.

88

When I Want a Gentle and Quiet Spirit

Do not let your adornment be
merely outward—arranging the hair,
wearing gold, or putting on
fine apparel—rather let it be
the hidden person of the heart,
with the incorruptible beauty
of a gentle and quiet spirit, which is
very precious in the sight of God.

1 PETER 3:3-4

IT'S GOOD TO TAKE CARE of yourself and make a consistent effort to always look good for your husband. But while you tend to your health and do what you should to stay attractive to him in what you wear and how you care for your skin and hair, you cannot neglect your inner self, where your lasting and ever-increasing beauty is found. The Bible says that the beauty of a gentle and quite spirit cannot be lost and is always pleasing to God.

Having a quiet spirit doesn't mean you barely talk above a whisper. God has given you a voice, and He intends for you to use it. But it is the quiet and peaceful spirit *behind* your voice that communicates you are not in an internal uproar. A gentle spirit doesn't mean you are weak. It means that you aren't brash, obnoxious, or rude. It means you are godly in nature and have love and respect for the people around you. What is in your heart shows on your face. The attractiveness of inner peace and gentleness *in* you will always manifest as beauty externally as well. And that is appealing to everyone—especially your husband.

Pray that God's Spirit in you will be the most important part of who you are, and that you will reflect the beauty of the Lord, which is beyond compare. His gentle and quiet Spirit in you will be more attractive to others than anything else.

My Prayer to God

LORD, I pray You would give me a gentle and quiet spirit, which I know is precious in Your sight. Enable me to have the inner beauty that is incorruptible, which comes from Your Spirit of peace dwelling in me. Only You can fill me with all I need in order to become as You want me to be. Show me how to always be attractive to my husband in the way I dress and look, but more importantly, help me to remember and understand where true and lasting beauty comes from. Enable me to be perceived by him and others as beautiful because of Your beautiful reflection in me. Help me to never be offensive or undesirable to be around. Keep me from allowing anyone to bring out the worst in me.

Let the beauty of Your Spirit in me shine through and

above all the fleshly parts of me that I am still dealing with and trying to allow You to perfect. Fill my heart with Your love, peace, and joy so that they are what always show on my face. Pour Your Spirit *over* me and *in* me so that what is seen on my face is not anger, concern, worry, or sadness, but rather contentment, calm, peace, and happiness. I depend on You to accomplish this in me because I know I cannot achieve this on my own. I worship You, Lord, as the Savior, Restorer, and Beautifier of my life.

In Jesus' name I pray.

89

When He Needs to Provide for His Family

*If anyone does not provide for his own,
and especially for those of his household,
he has denied the faith and is
worse than an unbeliever.*

1 Timothy 5:8

EVERY NORMAL, LOVING HUSBAND and father wants to provide well for his family. So does every normal, loving wife and mother. But the rebuke is strong in this Scripture, saying that if a *man* doesn't provide for *his* family and household, *he* is worse than an unbeliever. This doesn't mean if he goes through tough times in his work and loses his job, or has financial difficulties, that he has deserted the faith. It means if a man is careless or unconcerned about providing for his family, or if he goes off and spends money only on himself and not on his wife and children, he is in no way following the Lord.

God expects a man to work hard in order to be a good provider. And when he does, God blesses his work with success. But this doesn't happen automatically. A husband and wife must pray for it. The Bible says, "You do not have because you do not ask" (James 4:2). However, if your husband won't ask, you can ask for him. You can pray that he will follow the Lord in all he does—every aspect of it.

Ask God to help your husband provide for his family. And if your husband goes through a time where he is unable to provide, pray that God will help him get back on his feet again. Pray that the Lord will enable you to help provide as well, in any way you can. Keep praying, because your prayers for your husband have more power than you know.

My Prayer to God

Lord, I pray You will enable my husband to provide for his family. Give him the ability and desire to do what is necessary in order to accomplish that. When there is no work for him in his desired field, open his eyes to other ways to bring in income. Open new doors of opportunity for him to walk through. Show him how to better use the skills You have given him, or to develop new ones he didn't even know he had. Help him to get better and better at what he does so that he is never put out to pasture or turned away from work. Enable him to be innovative and creative, and take away any pride in him that refuses to either ask for work or to let others know he needs more secure work.

I know You would not hold my husband responsible to provide for his family if You weren't going to enable him to do so. Whenever he struggles in that area, I pray he will turn to You for that ability and opportunity. Help him to never be careless or uncaring about that, but to always diligently seek to do what needs to be done. Whenever I have work that is better paying or more secure than his, I pray he will be thankful and not threatened. Help him to remember that we are a team and we support each other. Give him the confidence to know that You will always have good work for him to do, and he must seek it after he first seeks You.

In Jesus' name I pray.

90

When We Are Imprisoned by Our Own Contention

A brother offended is harder
to win than a strong city,
and contentions are like the bars of a castle.

PROVERBS 18:19

BEING CONTENTIOUS MEANS having a tendency to argue or quarrel. Offending someone can sometimes be a difficult aspect of a relationship to mend because some people refuse to forgive and forget or simply let things go. The more offenses that pile up in a marriage relationship, the more quarrelsome and imprisoned you both become. They become like bars laid across a castle door, locking each other out. You must never sit by and let this happen in your marriage.

You don't want either you or your husband to ever wander the cold, dark halls of isolation. You both need the warmth of love, compassion, understanding, and togetherness in order to survive. That's why you must pray that any and all contentiousness between you and your husband be dissolved immediately by the power of the Holy Spirit.

If there is no contention between you and your husband now, pray that there never will be any in your future. Ask God to help you both avoid committing offenses against each other, with each subsequent offense placing another bar on the castle door. You not only end up locking the other person out, but also locking yourself in. And eventually these bars can be nearly impossible to remove without outside help. Everything you do in your marriage must build up and not tear down, must liberate and not imprison. The Spirit of God in you can, and will, help you do both.

My Prayer to God

LORD, I pray that my husband and I will not allow a contentious spirit or attitude to flourish in us. Keep us from committing offenses that hurt or anger each other. Help us to not be oversensitive, and therefore unable to let careless words or thoughtless actions roll off our backs. Teach us to forgive quickly and let go of things we might hold against each other. Enable us to rise above our insecurities and weaknesses, and refuse to fall prey to this trap of the enemy for our demise. Help us refuse to entertain any evil spirit of contention that rises up between us.

Where we have allowed our flesh to give place to, or make room for, a contentious and argumentative spirit between us, I confess that before You as sin. I ask You to forgive us and soften our hardened hearts. Where we have put bars on the castle door of our marriage that keep us separated and imprisoned, I pray You would dissolve them so they can never be erected or established again. I know that it is "better to dwell in a corner of a housetop, than in a house shared with a contentious woman" (Proverbs 21:9). Help me to never be a woman that my husband wants to avoid. Draw us both over to Your way of relating to each other, where offenses are forgiven, released, and forgotten immediately. Thank You, Lord, that nothing is too hard for You—not even breaking down the bars on a castle door.

In Jesus' name I pray.

91

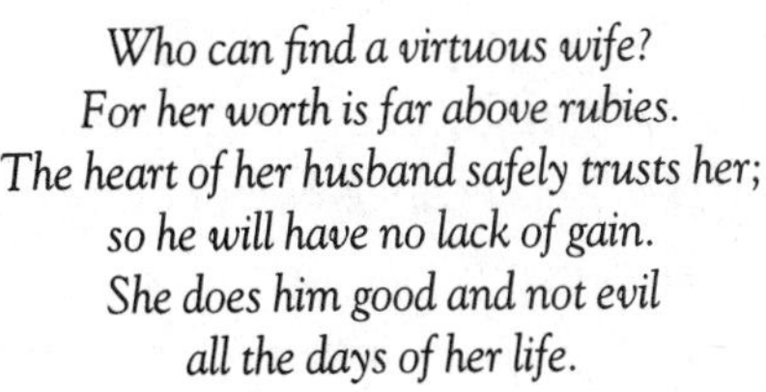

When I Want to Be a "Virtuous Wife"

Who can find a virtuous wife?
For her worth is far above rubies.
The heart of her husband safely trusts her;
so he will have no lack of gain.
She does him good and not evil
all the days of her life.

PROVERBS 31:10-12

THE EXAMPLE OF A VIRTUOUS WIFE in the Bible is inspiring to live up to, but you must not try this alone. You need the enablement of the Holy Spirit. First of all, the word "virtuous" means to live a morally excellent life. How can we do that without the righteousness of Jesus covering us? Being clothed in His righteousness, endowed with the perfect beauty of the Lord, and filled with the wisdom of the Holy Spirit are foundational steps for a virtuous life.

Once you have that foundation in the Lord, as you look to Him and depend on His power, He helps you to become the woman you want to be. That is, He teaches you to successfully manage a home, to be wise with money, and to develop useful skills so you are never sitting around doing nothing. He teaches you to not *rely* on physical beauty, because you now have the excellent beauty of the Holy Spirit in you. But you don't neglect your appearance, either. You take care of yourself and make an effort to stay healthy, strong, and attractive. These ideas and suggestions are found in the last half of Proverbs 31, and it is good to read that section of Scripture from time to time as a reminder—not of something you have to live up to, but of something God will help you attain.

Ask God to help you become a "virtuous wife." The promise is that when you do, your husband will always think of you as a blessing in his life. Being a "virtuous wife" doesn't mean becoming boring. It means becoming dynamic and full of life because you have the power of His Spirit in you. It will be the Lord's beauty and perfection shining through you that is irresistible.

My Prayer to God

Lord, I want to be like the "virtuous wife" described in Your Word (Proverbs 31:10-31). Help me to be trustworthy so that there is "no lack of gain" for my husband and me. Teach me to be wise with money and to work diligently to help provide for our family. Help me to give to those in need, and to prepare for the future so that we won't ever need to fear it.

I pray I will be an asset to my husband and will contribute to his good reputation. Enable me to develop marketable skills I can use to help bring in finances. Help me to be kind with the words I speak to him and to others so that I am always a blessing to them. I especially pray that because I reverence You, Lord, my husband will see Your beauty in me. Bless all the work I do, and may the fruit of my hands inspire the respect and admiration of my husband.

I ask You to be in charge of my life, for I know I cannot do everything right without Your miraculous enablement. Every day I pray You will help me do something good for my husband, something good for my home, something good for my children, something good for others, and something good for myself. Help me to do good and not evil all the days of my life.

In Jesus' name I pray.

92

When He Needs to Speak Well-Chosen Words

A soft answer turns away wrath, but a harsh word stirs up anger. The tongue of the wise uses knowledge rightly, but the mouth of fools pours forth foolishness.

PROVERBS 15:1-2

HOW MUCH DAMAGE has been done to others by the words certain people have spoken to them? How much hurt has been inflicted on *you* by the thoughtless, careless, or inconsiderate words of another person? How many times have ill-chosen words you or your husband said to each other stirred up hurt or discontent in your marriage? If he would have given you "a soft answer" instead of "a harsh word"—or if you would have said accepting words instead of rejecting words to him—how much better would your relationship be?

Ask God to help you be wise and not foolish with your words at all times, but especially with what you say to your husband. And if it is you who is the frequent recipient of hurtful words from your husband, pray that he will not foolishly tear down his marriage with speech that destroys. Pray that God will give him a softened heart, out of which pours words that build up and not tear down.

Ask God to help you make your first reaction to any harsh words your husband says not be more harsh words, but rather the soft answer that turns away wrath. This can only come from a heart softened by the Holy Spirit, which happens by spending time in God's presence and letting Him soak you through and through with His love. Pray your husband's heart will be tenderized in that same manner, and he will learn to choose his words well.

My Prayer to God

LORD, I pray You would fill my husband afresh with Your Holy Spirit today, so that the words coming out of his mouth will be kind and well-chosen. I know we both have the capacity to say words to each other that are harsh, insensitive, or hurtful. Whatever is in us that causes us to carelessly say something that foolishly tears down the foundation of our marriage instead of building it up, burn it out of our hearts by the power of Your Holy Spirit. Take away our selfishness, pettiness, unkindness, or carelessness, and fill us full of Your love, peace, and joy so that these are what overflow in our words.

Give my husband and me kind, compassionate, and thoughtful words that speak life, hope, and positive anticipation of the future. Help us not to think only of protecting ourselves, but rather to consider each other first. When we need to apologize to each other for words already spoken, free us to do that. Where my husband should speak positive words to replace any negative words he has spoken to me, that are still resounding in my mind, enable him to do that. But even if he doesn't, I pray You will erase every hurtful word still hanging in the air so that my memory is of good and not evil. Teach him to speak gentle words to me. Help me to always have a soft answer that "turns away wrath" for him.

In Jesus' name I pray.

93

When We Must Stand Strong

When the whirlwind passes by,
the wicked is no more, but the righteous
has an everlasting foundation.

Proverbs 10:25

When we walk with the Lord, living His way, depending on Him, praying to Him, and worshipping only Him, we are able to stand firm and not fall, no matter what is happening in our lives. Paul instructs us to be watchful and "stand fast in the faith, be brave, be strong" (1 Corinthians 16:13). He said to stand in what we know is true of God (Hebrews 2:1), and to "stand fast" in all we have been taught (2 Thessalonians 2:15). He warned us to stand knowing we could fall if we are not careful (1 Corinthians 10:12). He also said to "stand fast" in the freedom we have in Christ and not become "entangled again with a yoke of bondage" (Galatians 5:1).

Standing strong is something you *decide* to do. It wouldn't have been mentioned so many times in His Word if it wasn't necessary to address this stance in our lives. The success of your life and your marriage depend on both of you being able to stand strong in what is right—and in what you know of the Lord. Ask God to help you do your part by being watchful, by standing fast in faith, by reading His Word, by asking Him to lead you, and by standing strong in obedience to His ways. The Bible says, "The righteous will come through trouble" (Proverbs 12:13). Pray that God will enable you both to live righteous lives.

Ask God to help you stand for what is right and against evil. Ask Him to help you stand unified, and when you have decisions to make, to stand in the counsel of God (Isaiah 46:10). Most of all, ask God to enable you to stand strong in every situation.

My Prayer to God

Lord, I pray You would help my husband and me to stand strong in all we know of You, in all we read in Your Word, and in all You have taught us. Help us to stand firm in faith, love, peace, and purpose. Keep us standing on solid rock in good times and in bad. Thank You that Your promise to those of us who live Your way is that we will come successfully through difficult times (Proverbs 12:13). Thank You for Your Word that says because we are Your children, when we go through storms in our lives we will be able to stand firm while others fall (Proverbs 10:25).

Teach us to stand in Your truth at all times so that we won't drift away (Hebrews 2:1). We want to stand in awe of only You and Your Word, and not of the world and its enticements (Psalm 119:161). Help us to be unified, knowing that a house divided against itself cannot stand (Mark 3:25). Enable us to not get carried away by fear and doubt when hard things happen in our lives or in the world around us. Help us both to "count it all joy" when we go through trials, knowing You will perfect us in them as we depend on Your enabling power. We choose to find our strength in You in order to stand strong today and every day.

In Jesus' name I pray.

94

When I Have Anger in My Heart

Cease from anger, and forsake wrath;
do not fret—it only causes harm.

PSALM 37:8

EVERYONE BECOMES ANGRY about something sometimes, but you are not allowed to give anger permanent residence in your heart. That's because anger will burn a hole in your soul that will fill up with bitterness and unforgiveness, and it will seep through your personality until you become not only toxic to yourself but also to others around you. Anger festers in each one of us like an infected sore that quickly progresses to something far more serious every day it is allowed to remain unattended. In fact, God doesn't want us to even entertain it overnight. "Be angry, and do not sin: do not let the sun go down on your wrath" (Ephesians 4:26). That means we must not take it to bed with us, because it is doing more damage than we realize every moment we give it a place within us. You can *get* angry, but you must not *stay* angry. We are foolish to let anger stay in our heart (Ecclesiastes 7:9).

If you have unresolved anger, ask God to help you refuse its rule in your soul. Even if you feel your anger is justified, pray to be rid of it. If you are angry at your husband, remember that your ultimate battle is not with him. Even if he has done something thoughtless or hurtful, he is still not your enemy. It is hard to remember that when you are in the midst of a difficult situation.

Even if your anger is directed at others, you must get rid of it because it will show up in your face and in your personality, and it will negatively affect your marriage. When you are slow to anger, you are wise like the Lord (Psalm 103:8). Ask God to make you wise enough to "forsake all wrath" and avoid the harm it causes.

My Prayer to God

Lord, I pray You would take away all anger in me. No matter what reason I have for being angry, I know You don't want me to keep it in my heart. I pray You would help me to lay it down before You and let it go. Your Word says not to let the sun go down on my wrath. I absolutely do not want any wrath to fester in me and grow into an infected wound. I confess any long-term anger as sin, and I release it into Your hands. I know You are greater than the situation that is disturbing to me, so I ask You to help me trust You completely in this. I believe You will protect me in it so that I don't have to fight this battle.

Change my heart from anger to peace, from wrath to

release. Work in this situation and make it right. I know that an angry person is not good to be around, and I don't want to be that kind of person (Proverbs 22:24). Plant Your love, peace, and joy in my heart to flourish there instead. Your Word says we should not rush to be angry because "anger rests in the bosom of fools" (Ecclesiastes 7:9). Help me to be wise and not foolish, and be slow to anger just as You are (Psalm 103:8). I know that anger is a work of the flesh, so I pray You will enable me to walk in the Spirit in all I do (Romans 8:4).

In Jesus' name I pray.

95

When He Has Temptation Invading His Mind

You have heard that it was said to those of
old, "You shall not commit adultery."
But I say to you that whoever looks at a woman to
lust for her has already committed adultery with her
in his heart. If your right eye
causes you to sin, pluck it out and cast it
from you; for it is more profitable
for you that one of your members perish,
than for your whole body to be cast into hell.

MATTHEW 5:27-29

A SPIRIT OF SEXUAL LUST is so pervasive in our culture that we don't have to go searching for it; it comes to us. A man is wired to be susceptible because it enters through his eyes and the immodesty he sees. His mind can be invaded as he watches TV and films, by what he sees on the Internet, and even certain window displays in some stores. It is his responsibility to reject all that out of his mind. If a woman approaches him at work to flirt, he must remember who he is and turn away from her. That's why he needs your support in prayer.

Even if your husband never *intends* to entertain the idea of acting on sexual temptation, the thought in his mind can cause sin to enter his heart. It has to be stopped at the thought level. Your prayers can help him be strong enough to resist it. A threat *from* hell, like sexual temptation, can put him *through* hell if he doesn't get away from it immediately. Pray that all sexual temptation will be taken away from him and that this ploy of the enemy will not succeed.

Even if you don't think your husband would ever allow temptation to get the best of him, pray anyway. Most husbands will not tell their wives what they are experiencing along those lines. The struggle is real and you cannot ignore it. Pray for God to protect him and give him the strength he needs to stand in opposition to it.

My Prayer to God

Lord, I pray that sexual temptation will not find a place in my husband's mind, for You have said that even looking at a woman with thoughts of lust means a man has committed adultery in his heart. I pray that any attack of the enemy upon his mind in regard to this will be stopped immediately. Take away the source of temptation, whether it's a person or an image he has seen. Give him wisdom to recognize it as a trap to destroy his life. Give him the strength to reject it.

Show me how I can build up my husband in every way by showing appreciation, interest, desire, and support. Show me how to keep him fulfilled in his mind, heart, and body so that he isn't out in the world empty and exposed to the spirit of lust that infects it. Help me to not withhold myself from him in any way, for I know that displeases not only him but You as well. Give him the commitment of heart to honor our marriage in every way. Keep him from entertaining a secret life, even in his mind. Bring to light all lustful thoughts and help him to reject them. Reveal to me anything I need to see, and show me how to pray specifically. Free us from this enemy invasion.

In Jesus' name I pray.

96

When We Desire the Crown of Life

Blessed is the man who endures temptation;
for when he has been approved,
he will receive the crown of life
which the Lord has promised
to those who love Him.

JAMES 1:12

GOD'S PROMISE IS to give us "the crown of life" when we endure all kinds of temptation. That means resisting temptation must become a way of life. And in these times and in our society, there are few places we can go to avoid being tempted. We are faced with temptation to look at things we shouldn't and do things we must not do. We all have the enemy of our soul searching through our weaknesses in order to find a way to destroy us. We have our own desires drawing us away from

God and His ways. With the world, our flesh, and the devil constantly working against us, we must be extra vigilant in prayer.

We all have some susceptibility or insecurity that makes us vulnerable to temptation of some kind, and it can overwhelm us at any time. But we can fortify ourselves daily in the Lord in order to resist it. The reward for resisting temptation is that we receive God's blessings and long life. We also ultimately receive the crown of life for eternity. This is the greatest incentive, for who doesn't want that?

You and your husband want to receive all God has for you. So pray that God will help you both stand strong in resisting every temptation to do, think, or say anything that you know doesn't please Him. Specifically name before Him the areas where you are most tempted to stray from His best for you. Ask Him to take away all desire for anything that doesn't add to your life, and replace it with a desire to do only that which glorifies Him.

My Prayer to God

LORD, I pray You would take away all temptation in my husband's life, and in my life as well. Remove any ungodly desires we have and help us to resist them. I know the enemy of our souls works to destroy us through temptation to violate Your laws, so I pray You would strengthen us to resist him at all times and in all places. Keep us from having weak moments and succumbing to them. Put impenetrable layers of Your protection around us, so that the temptations of the culture that are so readily accessible cannot penetrate our hearts, minds, and souls.

Reveal areas of temptation we are not seeing that can become a threat to us in the future. Open our eyes and keep us undeceived. Help us to see Your truth in every situation so that we don't fall unwittingly into any traps. Enable us to spot the pitfalls before we come close to stumbling into them. Where either of us has fallen into temptation of any kind, I pray we would confess that before You, repent of it, be forgiven, and set free. Deliver us from the tempter and enable us to stand strong against all that is not Your will for our lives. Help us to stay on the path You have for us each hour of every day, knowing we will receive "the crown of life" as Your reward when we do.

In Jesus' name I pray.

97

When I Want God's Love to Be Seen in Me

Beloved, let us love one another,
for love is of God;
and everyone who loves is
born of God and knows God.
He who does not love does not
know God, for God is love.

1 JOHN 4:7-8

HOW MANY TIMES have we heard someone going through a divorce say, "We just fell out of love with each other"? True and lasting love is not a condition people fall in and out of, depending on the circumstances. A person may fall in love, but it's not *true* love until a commitment is made.

The kind of love that makes a marriage work is sustained by God when an effort is made to commit to keeping love alive and growing deeper. That takes having the love of God in us, and it takes prayer. Because on those days when you don't *feel* love—and even the greatest loving couples have times when they don't *feel* love—you still have to *show* love. True love is not what you *feel* every moment of every day anyway; it's what you commit to, and what you seek God for more of than you have on your own. God's love is great and unconditional and unfailing. God's love keeps a marriage together when our own love fails.

We who know the Lord have the distinct advantage of being able to love our spouse at all times—even when we don't feel like it—because we are born of the God of love and His Holy Spirit of love resides within us. God's unconditional and unfailing love can override our feeble and fickle love—the love we can fall in and out of if something doesn't go the way we want. The love of God is fresh in you every day when you walk with Him. He can stir love *in* you that you didn't know you were capable of having. And His love *in* you will manifest *through* you at times when your human love loses strength.

My Prayer to God

Lord, I pray You would fill me with Your unfailing and unconditional love. I thank You that You are the God of love and Your Spirit of love dwells within me. Fill me afresh with Your love so that it overflows to others—especially my husband. I pray You would pour out Your Spirit on my husband today and fill him afresh with Your love as well. With the weakness, frailty, and fickleness of our human love—which too often relies on feelings, circumstances, and whims—I know we cannot make our marriage successful. We need *Your* love to be the driving force.

Only Your love doesn't waver. Only Your love forgives

human failures. It is Your love that enables our love for each other to grow deeper. I confess any time I have not felt loving toward my husband and my words and actions have conveyed that. I know this is not pleasing to You, and it is certainly not pleasing to him. Forgive me and help me to deliberately show love to him in ways he can clearly see and understand. Help us to feel love for each other even in difficult times between us. Enable me to get beyond my own needs and become a conduit of Your unfailing love to him. May Your love be seen in me at all times.

In Jesus' name I pray.

98

When He Needs Healing

Is anyone among you suffering?
Let him pray...Is anyone among you sick?
Let him call for the elders of the church,
and let them pray over him, anointing him
with oil in the name of the Lord. And the
prayer of faith will save the sick,
and the Lord will raise him up.

JAMES 5:13-15

IT IS ALWAYS UPSETTING when a family member is sick, and especially so when it is the head of the household who provides for the family. You don't want to see your husband suffer, and especially not if it is a serious illness. So when he is sick you must pray *with* him and *for* him about his healing, even if he is a nonbeliever.

God refers to Himself as Yahweh-Rapha, which means "the

Lord who heals." It is His nature to heal, and we can find healing in His presence. If Jesus didn't intend to heal us, why does the Bible say He came as the healer? He didn't just do it for the disciples or the people at that time; He did it for now. He is the Lord who "heals all your diseases" (Psalm 103:3). He is the Savior, who "by His stripes we are healed" (Isaiah 53:5). He is "the Sun of Righteousness" who arises "with healing in His wings" (Malachi 4:2). He "is the same yesterday, today, and forever" (Hebrews 13:8). It is not Jesus *was* the healer; it's Jesus *is* the healer. And it's not "if you would have been around when He was on earth in the flesh, you maybe could have been healed too." It's "by his wounds you have been healed" (1 Peter 2:24 NIV).

Healing doesn't always happen immediately, so if you pray and nothing happens, don't give up. As to why some are healed and some are not, that is God's business. Just because people prayed and a person wasn't healed doesn't mean God never heals and so we should stop praying for healing. It means we pray and trust God for *His* answer, whatever that is. Praying is not telling God what to do. It's telling Him our desires and trusting Him to answer according to His will.

My Prayer to God

LORD, I thank You that You are the Lord who heals us (Exodus 15:26). Thank You that You are Yahweh-Rapha, and it is Your nature to heal and make us whole. I pray You would touch my husband with Your healing power and make him whole. Show him if this sickness is caused by something he has done or not done with regard to taking care of himself. If he has not lived Your way and he is paying for it now, reveal that to him so he can correct his actions. Give him the knowledge, wisdom, and understanding he needs in order to do the right thing and treat his body in the proper way so that nothing hinders the healing You have for him.

If necessary, lead him to the right doctor who can make the correct diagnosis and prescribe the proper treatment. Show me how I can help him recover. I know our life is in Your hands, and it is You who sustains us and meets us on our sickbed to heal us. Thank You, Jesus, that by Your stripes we are healed, and You are healing my husband. Whenever and however the healing manifests, we are grateful for it. Increase his faith to believe in Your Word and Your ability and desire to heal him.

In Jesus' name I pray.

99

When We Must Become Like-Minded

If there is any consolation in Christ, if any comfort of love, if any fellowship of the Spirit, if any affection and mercy, fulfill my joy by being like-minded, having the same love, being of one accord, of one mind.

PHILIPPIANS 2:1-2

IN ANY MARRIAGE when the husband and wife are in the midst of busy careers, raising children, pursuing separate interests, and various other involvements, they can end up leading separate lives and growing apart. This may seem like an impossibility to you in the beginning of your lives together, but it can happen subtly without you even realizing it. Think about how many times we have heard divorcing couples say, "We just grew apart." That doesn't have to happen. We aren't destined to grow apart. We grow as we choose to. Growing apart happens when there are unresolved disagreements between you. The two of you begin to feel as if you are always in opposition, and this sets the stage for communication breakdown.

You and your husband must always be convinced that you are on the same team and not in competition with each other. You need to feel that you have the same ultimate goals and direction in life. You should be able to agree more than you disagree. You don't have to be attached at the hip, but you must have an attachment of the mind. You should be able to work things out and "be perfectly joined together in the same mind" (1 Corinthians 1:10). Of course, that means having the mind of Christ. But that doesn't just happen, either.

You have the mind of Christ when you receive Jesus, but you have to *let* His mind be in you (Philippians 2:5). That means you can choose *not* to. It's the same as having access to God's power and choosing not to plug into it. The way you and your husband become like-minded is to *choose* to have the mind of Christ and the love of God in you.

My Prayer to God

Lord, I pray my husband and I will grow more together every day and not apart. Help us to see the things that separate us or drive a wedge between us. Enable us to have the same mind. Thank You that You have given us the mind of Christ. Help us to daily welcome and embrace that connecting of mind and spirit with Yours. Where we have in any way gone our separate ways, I pray You would bring us back together on the same path. Help us to be like-minded so that we do not allow anything to come between us.

Enable us to always choose to be on the same team and not on opposite sides. Where we disagree on serious matters, help us to find our common ground in You. Help us to always choose Your way over our own. Teach us to choose each other and our marriage over anything else. I pray we will bring You joy by being "like-minded, having the same love, being of one accord, of one mind" (Philippians 2:2). I pray that You, "the God of patience and comfort" will enable us "to be like-minded toward one another, according to Christ Jesus," so that we may "with one mind and one mouth glorify" You, Lord (Romans 15:5-6).

In Jesus' name I pray.

100

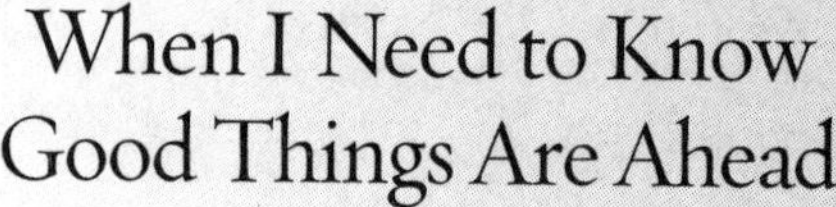

When I Need to Know Good Things Are Ahead

Eye has not seen, nor ear heard,
nor have entered into the heart of man
the things which God has prepared
for those who love Him…
Now we have received, not the spirit of
the world, but the Spirit who is from God,
that we might know the things that have
been freely given to us by God.

1 Corinthians 2:9,12

The Bible says God has more for us than we can imagine. Sometimes we let our sights become so low that we can't imagine much. We think if we can just survive this challenging situation we are in, it will be a miracle. There are other times, however, when we can imagine so much that it's amazing to think God could possibly have more for us than that. The truth is that no matter what we are going through, we always have something to look forward to because God is in control of our lives. In fact, when we go to be with the Lord, we are going to be amazed that we worried so much and prayed so little on earth.

As a wife, you need to have an understanding deep in your heart that there is always hope, no matter what the challenges are, no matter how difficult the impasse, no matter how hopeless things may seem. But it takes the Holy Spirit of God *in* you to help you comprehend the great things ahead. And without the Holy Spirit, you can't receive all God has for you.

When you welcome the working of the Holy Spirit in you, it opens up your life for blessings—both individually and as a couple—beyond what you can possibly see now. In the Lord, the best is yet to come, even though there are many times when that seems impossible to imagine. As you continue to stay close to God in prayer and worship, and continue to trust Him for each day, He will speak to your heart about the good things ahead for you.

My Prayer to God

LORD, I pray You would give me a vision beyond myself and my limitations—beyond what I can see or imagine—so that I can grow in understanding of all You have for me in this life and the next. Bestow upon me a new gift of faith in Your Word and a greater understanding of its meaning. Enable me to receive a revelation that assures me I am never without hope, no matter what the situation. Thank You that You have more for me and my husband than we can imagine.

Lift my eyes from my struggles and challenges, and help me to focus on You and Your promises. Let hope rise in my heart because I trust in You. No matter what kind of impasse my husband and I may face, no matter how limited our own perspective, there is no impasse in Your kingdom, and Your perspective is unlimited. Help us to see that, even when we have a struggle between us and cannot imagine how it can ever be resolved, You have the solution and will bring it to pass as we look to You in prayer and surrender to Your will. Now to You, who are "able to do exceedingly abundantly above all that we ask or think, according to the power that works in us," to You, Lord, be all glory today and forever (Ephesians 3:20).

In Jesus' name I pray.

OTHER BOOKS *by* STORMIE OMARTIAN

Lead Me, Holy Spirit

Stormie has written books on prayer that have helped millions of people talk to God. Now she focuses on the Holy Spirit and how He wants you to listen to His gentle leading when He speaks to your heart, soul, and spirit. He wants to help you enter into the relationship with God you yearn for and the wholeness and freedom He has for you. He wants to lead you into a better life than you could ever possibly live without Him.

Prayer Warrior

Stormie says, "A war is already going on around you, and you are in it whether you want to be or not. This is a spiritual war of good and evil—between God and His enemy—and God wants us to stand strong on His side, the side that wins. We win the war when we pray in power because prayer *is* the battle." This book will help you become a powerful prayer warrior who understands the path to victory.

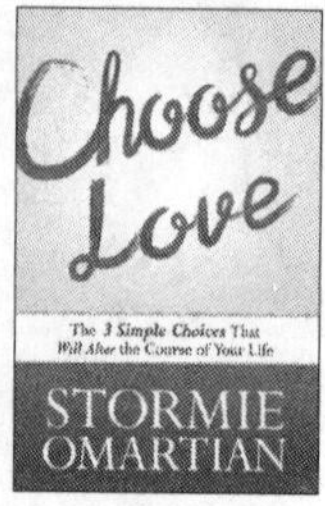

Choose Love

We reflect God most clearly when we are motivated by the power of love in all we say and do. But first we have to understand the depth of God's love for us and receive it. Then we must learn how to effectively express our love for Him. Transform your heart, your relationships, and your future as you press into God's love and let the power of His life and character move through you.

The Power of Praying® for Your Adult Children

"Our concern for our children doesn't stop once they step out in the world and leave home. If anything it increases," says Stormie. "There is much more to be concerned about, but as parents we have less influence over their lives than ever. Even so, there is a way to make a big difference in their lives every day, and that is through prayer." This book will help every parent to pray powerfully for their adult children and find peace in the process.

To learn more about Harvest House books and to read sample chapters, log on to our website:

www.harvesthousepublishers.com